MAKERS
of the
MUSLIM
WORLD

Shah ‘Abbas

TITLES IN THE MAKERS OF THE MUSLIM WORLD SERIES

Series Editor: Patricia Crone, Institute for Advanced Study, Princeton

Abd al-Ghani al-Nabulusi, Samer Akkach
'Abd al-Malik, Chase F. Robinson
Abd al-Rahman III, Maribel Fierro
Abu Nuwas, Philip Kennedy
Ahmad al-Mansur, Mercedes García-Arenal
Ahmad ibn Hanbal, Christopher Melchert
Ahmad Riza Khan Barelwi, Usha Sanyal
Akbar, André Wink
Al-Ma'mun, Michael Cooperson
Al-Mutanabbi, Margaret Larkin
Amir Khusraw, Sunil Sharma
Ashraf 'Ali Thanawi, Muhammad Qasim Zaman
Chinggis Khan, Michal Biran
El Hajj Beshir Agha, Jane Hathaway
Fazlallah Astarabadi and the Hurufis, Shazad Bashir
Ghazali, Eric Ormsby
Hasan al-Banna, Gudrun Krämer
Husain Ahmad Madani, Barbara Metcalf
Ibn 'Arabi, William C. Chittick
Ibn Fudi, Ahmad Dallal
Ikhwan al-Safa, Godefroid de Callatay
Imam Shafi'i, Kecia Ali
Karim Khan Zand, John R. Perry
Mehmed Ali, Khaled Fahmy
Mu'awiya ibn abi Sufyan, R. Stephen Humphreys
Muhammad Abduh, Mark Sedgwick
Mulla Sadra, Sayeh Meisami
Nasser, Joel Gordon
Nazira Zeineddine, Miriam Cooke
Sa'di, Homa Katouzian
Shaykh Mufid, Tamima Bayhom-Daou
Usama ibn Munqidh, Paul M. Cobb

For current information and details of other books in the series, please visit www.oneworld-publications.com

MAKERS
of the
MUSLIM
WORLD

Shah 'Abbas

The King Who Refashioned Iran

SHOLEH A. QUINN

ONEWORLD

SHAH ‘ABBAS

A Oneworld Book

Published by Oneworld Publications 2015

A CIP record for this title is available
from the British Library

ISBN 978-1-85168-425-0
eISBN 978-1-78074-568-8

Typeset by Jayvee, Trivandrum, India
Printed and bound by
CPI Group (UK) Ltd, Croydon, CR0 4YY

Oneworld Publications
10 Bloomsbury Street,
London WC1B 3SR, England

Attributed to Bishndas
Portrait of Shah ʻAbbas I, ca. 1617
Ink and opaque watercolor on paper; 19.5 × 15.6 cm ($7\frac{11}{16} \times 6\frac{1}{8}$ in.)
Harvard Art Museums/Arthur M. Sackler Museum, Gift of Stuart Cary Welch, Jr., 1999.304
Photo: Imaging Department © President and Fellows of Harvard College

To my husband
Stephen N. Lambden

CONTENTS

ACKNOWLEDGEMENTS

A number of friends and colleagues provided assistance with various aspects of this project. I am grateful to Patricia Crone, the series editor, for inviting me to write this volume. She read the first two chapters of the manuscript and gave careful critical feedback before illness prevented her from doing more. I very much appreciate her time and assistance. Rudi Matthee read the entire manuscript twice and provided very helpful comments and suggestions. Ernest Tucker also kindly read the manuscript and gave me very good advice. Of course I take full responsibility for all errors and oversights. In addition to those who read the manuscript, Novin Doostdar and Juliet Mabey, of Oneworld Publications, were always encouraging, and James Magniac and Laura McFarlane of Oneworld provided much helpful guidance and assistance. I am grateful to Kathleen McCully for her careful copyediting of the manuscript. I also thank Mary McWilliam and staff of the Arthur M. Sackler Museum, Harvard University Art Museums, for helping me obtain the drawing of Shah 'Abbas for the frontispiece of this book.

A number of friends and colleagues provided encouragement, moral support, and/or assistance during the course of preparing this volume: Susan Amussen, Shahzad Bashir, Kate Campbell, Massumeh Farhad, Marvin Fletcher, Katherine Jellison, Ruth Mostern, Kurt Schnier, and Mark Stein. I never would have completed this volume without my family. My parents, Robert and Manijeh Quinn, were always supportive and encouraging, as were my sister Laleh Quinn and her partner, Doug Nitz. Both my father and sister read the manuscript as non-specialist readers and offered helpful suggestions. Finally, my husband, Stephen Lambden, also read the entire manuscript and gave me wonderful feedback. I cannot thank him enough for his constant emotional support and kindness, and for always generously sharing his vast knowledge, even in times of poor health.

PREFACE

Shah 'Abbas ruled Iran when the Safavid dynasty was at the peak of its power. He is considered one of the most influential kings in the history of Iran. His name, which often has the title "the great" attached to it, is synonymous with Isfahan, one of the best loved cities in Iran. He is a figure about whom Iranians still relate stories. All of this makes writing his biography a challenging task indeed. That this larger-than-life king ruled for some forty-two years makes it even more difficult to condense his life into a very short introductory volume.

Shah 'Abbas has received considerable scholarly attention already. In the 1950s, Nasr Allah Falsafi, scholar of Iranian history, wrote a five-volume biography of the king, a monumental Persian work that is still cited today. More recently, in 2009, an exhibit specifically devoted to Shah 'Abbas at the British Museum brought with it the publication of an edited volume of essays mostly relating to Shah 'Abbas and the arts, to say nothing of an array of souvenirs, including Shah 'Abbas t-shirts, coffee cups, ball-point pens, and refrigerator magnets. The same year, David Blow's detailed biography, *Shah 'Abbas: the Ruthless King Who Became an Iranian Legend*, was published. Shah 'Abbas had entered the minds of the public.

So compelling a figure is Shah 'Abbas that even general survey works on the Safavid dynasty tend to devote most of their pages to him, often at the expense of other kings deemed less "important." Furthermore, countless specialized articles have been written, particularly in the last two decades, about different aspects of Shah 'Abbas's reign, covering everything from his diplomatic relations with specific parts of the world to religious and philosophical movements. Finally, the ongoing *Encyclopaedia Iranica* project continues to publish, both in print and online, articles that often reflect the newest, the best, and sometimes the only scholarship on Iran-related topics. I have made particular use of this valuable resource for this study.

In the pages that follow, I have attempted to cover some of the most important aspects of his reign: the circumstances under which he came to power, his consolidation of power after becoming king, his defeat of internal and external enemies, the establishment of a capital city in Isfahan, and some of the political and cultural developments that took place.

As part of the Makers of the Muslim World series, this volume is written primarily for a general audience of non-specialists. It is not by any means a comprehensive biography of Shah 'Abbas's entire career. Rather, I have chosen to focus on significant and representative events, developments, and facets of his life. In some cases, I have provided detailed descriptions of a particular event in order to illustrate more general trends. In doing this, I hope to provide the reader with a sense of how Shah 'Abbas dealt with specific situations within a larger context. The length of his rule, in contrast with the length of this volume, means that I have had to leave out many things. Readers who are interested in learning more about this fascinating king will find suggestions for further reading in the bibliography.

I have chosen to divide this book both chronologically and thematically. Chapter 1 provides historical background, and chapter 2 covers the early years of his life and the first phase of his reign, 1571–1598, when he defeated his internal and external enemies and consolidated his power, prior to moving the Safavid capital to Isfahan. Chapters 3–6 each cover aspects of the second phase of his rule from 1598 to 1612, including the building of Isfahan, religious developments, warfare and diplomacy, and the arts. Chapter 7 examines the final phase of his reign from 1612 to 1629, when he spent much of his time in the northern Caspian Sea region, and provides some brief concluding remarks. In a few cases, events taking place after 1612 appear in earlier chapters for the purposes of continuity.

I have tried to quote from a fairly wide range of primary sources. While these references do not even come close to representing the huge amount of material available for Shah 'Abbas, they do provide the reader with a sense of the range of material available for the consideration of his life.

ABBREVIATIONS

The following abbreviations are used in the references found in the text and bibliography. Full references to these works appear in the bibliography:

Carmelites:	*A Chronicle of the Carmelites*, 2 vols
Della Valle:	*Pietro Della Valle*, Italian edition/English translation
CHIr:	*Cambridge History of Iran*, vol. 6
EIR:	*Encyclopaedia Iranica* online
EI2:	*Encyclopedia of Islam*, second edition, online
TAA:	*Iskandar Beg Munshi, Tarikh-i alam-ara-yi 'Abbasi*, Persian edition/English translation

1

HISTORICAL BACKGROUND

THE SAFAVIDS: THE SUFI ORDER

Shah 'Abbas was the fifth monarch of the Safavid dynasty, which had ruled Iran since 1501. The history of this dynasty is one of the most fascinating in all of Islamic history, and Shah 'Abbas one of its most interesting rulers. One of the more unusual aspects of the dynasty is the fact that its founder was a Sufi leader. Sufism is the type of Islam that focuses on spirituality and it is in principle apolitical. Its aim is to achieve direct communication or even union with God, and to this end Sufis will engage in activities such as *zikr* (repeating a particular word or phrase), prayer, fasting, and other spiritual practices. Over time, Sufis came to believe that mystical union could only be achieved with the assistance of a spiritual guide, known as a *shaykh* or *pir*, and organizations known as Sufi orders headed by such guides came into existence. Mystically-oriented individuals would come together to study the spiritual way with a shaykh, and many others in the area would seek his advice or blessings, and lavish gifts on the organization. The wealth, prestige, and following of such a shaykh could be immense, and the position was in the process of becoming hereditary. In practice, then, Sufism was often far from apolitical. Sufi leaders acquired considerable political importance, especially in the chaotic conditions in Iran following the Mongol invasions of the thirteenth century.

The Safavids began as a traditional Sufi order. The founder was one Safi al-Din, "the pure one of the religion" (1252–1334), usually known as Shaykh Safi, and it is from his name that the Safavids derive theirs. The shaykh’s ancestors were members of a prominent family in Ardabil on the southwestern coast of the Caspian Sea. The first to be mentioned in surviving written sources, Firuz Shah “Zarrin Kulah” (“Golden Cap”), was a pastoralist, probably of Kurdish origin. His descendants were devout landowners and local men of influence who clashed from time to time with Georgian “infidels” who militarily threatened Ardabil.

According to Ibn Bazzaz, a contemporary of Shaykh Safi’s son who composed a massive hagiography entitled the *Safvat al-safa* (“Essence of Purity”), Shaykh Safi was a pious person who had visionary dreams, performed miracles, and led a devout, ascetic life. Instead of fighting Georgians, he went seeking a Sufi master, and after an exhaustive search, he met Shaykh Zahid Gilani. Shaykh Zahid, who became his spiritual teacher, was the founder of his own Sufi order. Shaykh Safi’s relationship with Shaykh Zahid was very close. He married the shaykh’s daughter, gave his own daughter in marriage to Shaykh Zahid’s son, and was even thought to have received instruction from him from beyond the grave. Shaykh Zahid had made it very clear during his lifetime that he wanted Shaykh Safi to be his successor. While this did not go over particularly well with his family (he had at least one son who could have taken over) or all of his followers, when he died, Shaykh Safi inherited his position and established the order in Ardabil. From this point on, the leadership of the order became hereditary. Successive descendants of Shaykh Safi gained power and prestige in the area, and as they did so, they came into contact with dynasties that controlled the neighboring regions. There were a fair number of such dynasties.

When the so-called Ilkhanid dynasty founded by the Mongols in Iran came to an end, in the late thirteenth and early fourteenth centuries, the regions they had controlled were divided up among a number of smaller rulers. Some hailed from nomadic Turkish tribesmen known as Turkomans, who had migrated to Iran together with the Mongols. The two most important dynasties founded by

Turkomans were picturesquely known as the "Black Sheep" (Qara Qoyunlu) and the "White Sheep" (Aq Qoyunlu) rulers – named perhaps for the color of sheep they raised – both of whom had their center in Tabriz when they were at the height of their power. There was also a minor Mongol dynasty known as the Jalayarids, and several other local or regional powers vying for territory and supremacy. In Anatolia, a small principality ruled by a family known as the Ottomans was quickly expanding and eventually shared a border with the Aq Qoyunlu. It was with the Black Sheep and the White Sheep that the Safavids came into contact. Both the Qara Qoyunlu and the Aq Qoyunlu intermarried with them, and regarded them as useful allies.

Shaykh Safi and his first three successors were rather typical shaykhs for their time, meaning that their followers engaged in standard Sufi activities such as prayer, fasting, and feeding the poor. The order was Sunni, but not partisan, if we are to trust the *Safvat al-safa*. One day, we are told, Shaykh Zahid was communicating with God. When his followers asked him where he had been, he said that his heart had traveled the entire world in order to choose an appropriate spot for a center led by Shaykh Safi, and he had decided upon Ardabil because the people were pure in their faith: "In this place, there has not been and [there still] is not any dispute or different sectarian opinions … *only* Sunna and jama'a [good Sunni practice and unity]" (Ibn Bazzaz, *Safvat*, 178). Here, the differentiation between Sunnism and Shi'ism was not as clear as it had sometimes been in the past, or as it is today. At the present time, Sunnis recognize four legitimate successors to the Prophet Muhammad: three companions and then 'Ali, his cousin and son-in-law. Shi'is, on the other hand, believe that 'Ali, as a family member, should have been the first successor to the Prophet. 'Ali was regarded as an imam and the religious authority, as were his descendants. Shi'is rarely enjoyed political power, as most Islamic ruling dynasties, with a few exceptions, have been Sunni. However, during the time of Shaykh Safi, Sunni Sufi orders often venerated 'Ali. But the Safavids were to swing in a Shi'i direction in a more drastic way.

With the accession of Safi's great-great-grandson Shaykh Junayd in 851/1447–1448, there were dramatic changes in the order's activities. First, the Sufis became involved in border warfare (*ghaza*) against the Byzantine territory in Trebizond, eastern Anatolia, and the Circassians in the Caucasus region, thereby adding militancy to their characteristics. Second, the order was coming to be distinguished by Shiʻism of the heterodox type known as *ghuluww* (exaggerated belief), encompassing (among other things) the belief that the divinity could manifest itself in select human beings. Junayd was seen as a divine figure by his followers. According to a contemporary, if hostile, source, they "openly called Shaykh Junayd 'god' and his son 'son of god'" (Khunji, *Amini*, 57/272).

FROM SUFI ORDER TO RULING DYNASTY

Another way in which the Safavids were unique is that, while not Turks themselves, they came to power by enlisting Turkish tribes in eastern Anatolia (now eastern Turkey). Turks had lived in Anatolia since the eleventh century, thanks to the Seljuq invasions, but many more had come in with the Mongols, and it was from among these tribes that the Safavids were now recruiting followers. This began under Shaykh Junayd, who spent a number of years wandering in Anatolia and Syria because he had been ousted from leadership of the order by a Qara Qoyunlu chief. Taking advantage of Aq Qoyunlu/Qara Qoyunlu rivalries, Junayd forged an alliance with the Aq Qoyunlu and married the sister of the Aq Qoyunlu ruler. Junayd's son Haydar, on the basis of a dream of the Imam ʻAli, created a uniform for his followers in the form of a red cap with twelve folds, representing the Twelve Shiʻi Imams. The Turkoman supporters who wore the Haydarian crown, or *taj-i Haydari*, came to be known as Qizilbash, or redheads. Initially pejorative, the term later dropped its negative associations. This distinctive cap can be seen in miniature paintings of the time, where Qizilbash warriors proudly donning their unique headgear dot the landscape in colorful battle and court scenes.

With the assistance of their Qizilbash supporters, Junayd and his successors, including his grandson, the handsome redhead Isma'il, raided and wrought havoc among the Christians and the local peasantries alike. Junayd and his son Haydar were killed in battle after experiencing both successes and failures, but in 1501 Isma'il succeeded in wresting Tabriz from his rivals, the Black Sheep. In Tabriz, in the words of an early chronicler, he proceeded to place "the crown of the caliphate and world conquest on his head" and then set out to subdue the rest of the country (Khvandamir, *Habib*, trans. v. 1, 576). At this point, the Sufi order had transformed itself into the dynasty from which Shah 'Abbas was descended.

Yet another way in which the Safavids were unique is that they imposed Shi'ism upon their subjects, the majority of whom were Sunni Muslims. There is no precedent for this. When, back in the tenth and early eleventh century, large parts of Iran were ruled by the Buyids, another Shi'ite dynasty from the Caspian coast, the Sunnis were left alone, and Shi'ite dynasties in other regions had also refrained from interfering with the faith of their Sunni subjects. The Safavid decision is all the more unique in that they themselves expressed *ghuluww*, or "exaggerated" Shi'ism, but what they imposed on their subjects turned out to be Twelver Shi'ism or Imamism, the much more standard form of Shi'ism which is the official religion of Iran today, in which there is no complete indwelling of the divine in human beings.

The *ghuluww* Shi'ism that the Safavids represented at the time is vividly illustrated in the poetry that Isma'il wrote before his accession under the pen-name Khata'i. Here he proclaims his own divinity and identifies himself as a re-appearance of past prophets, including Abraham, Jesus, and Muhammad, and of a plethora of pre-Islamic Persian kings, both mythical and real; he also seems to identify himself as the Mahdi, the savior figure who would return to make Shi'ism prevail on earth and regenerate the world.

> I am the living Khidr and Jesus son of Mary …
>
> (Minorsky, "Poetry," 1042a)
>
> Know for certain that Khata'i is of divine nature/that he is related to Muhammad Mustafa …
>
> (Minorsky, "Poetry," 1043a)
>
> I am Faridun, Khosrau, Jamshid, and Zohak. I am Zal's son (Rostam) and Alexander.
>
> (Minorsky, "Poetry," 1047a)
>
> By the Lord! Come and behold: God's light has reappeared;
> Muhammad Mustafa the Seal of Prophets has come!
>
> (Minorsky, "Poetry," 1048a)
>
> God's friend Abraham has put on a (new) garment and come to life. His name is Ismaʿil. Let souls be his sacrifice, for an appeal has come from God …
>
> The Mahdi's period has begun. The light of eternal life has dawned (upon) the world.
>
> (Minorsky, "Poetry," 1049a)

Early Safavid sources state that in 1501, after crowning himself, Ismaʿil had the Friday sermon (*khutba*) recited in the name of the guided or Twelve Imams because "the shah's entire concern was the propagation of the Imami sect and strengthening of the Prophet's law," thereby proclaiming Shiʿism as the official state religion and imposing this sect upon a country with a majority Sunni population. In addition to this, the muezzins were ordered to add the phrase "And I profess that ʿAli is the Friend of God" to the call to prayer, which also served to give his emergent state a distinctly Shiʿi religious identity (Khvandamir, *Habib* v. 4, 467). Ismaʿil's followers appear to have understood his coronation and the establishment of Shiʿism as commencing the Mahdi's reign, as Ismaʿil himself had stated in the poem quoted above: "the Mahdi's period has begun" (Arjomand, "Rise of Shah Esmaʿil," 4). The reasons for Shah Ismaʿil's decision to enforce Shiʿism are unclear, and while many suggestions have been offered as to why he did this, the answer remains elusive. What we do know is that in making his religious proclamation, Isma'il changed the course of Iran's history in a deep and profound way. In the long run the policy he initiated enjoyed almost total success; approximately ninety percent of Iran's population today is Shi'i.

After the Shi'i proclamation and coronation of 1501, Isma'il spent ten years conquering the rest of Iran and taking Baghdad. These were gritty, hard-fought campaigns that significantly expanded the Safavid state. However, the military successes ended when he suffered a dramatic loss to the rival Ottoman empire at Chaldiran in 1514. The Ottomans were worried about the increasing power of the Safavids because the Turkoman population of Ottoman eastern Anatolia subscribed to the same beliefs as the Qizilbash and they feared mass defection – large numbers of Turkomans had in fact joined Isma'il's cause – and even worse, they faced the possibility of losing eastern Anatolia to the Safavids. This is what led to the Battle of Chaldiran. The Ottoman army had superior weaponry and far outnumbered the Safavids, who suffered heavy casualties and lost a large number of high-ranking Qizilbash. The victory gave the Ottomans control over eastern Anatolia.

As for Shah Isma'il, he never recovered from the defeat, which ruined both his own belief and that of his followers in his divinity. Whereas previously, according to at least one traveler's account, his adherents had gone into battle without armor, believing that they were divinely protected, now Shah Isma'il himself went into semi-retirement, seeking oblivion in drink and opium, and while the story that he never smiled again may be apocryphal, it is certainly apt (Grey, "Travels," 206). Interestingly, legends about Shah Isma'il, including his claims to divinity, made their way to Europe – even during his lifetime and as early as 1501 – where he was viewed with hope as a pro-Christian potential ally against the Ottoman empire. Shah Isma'il died ten years after the Battle of Chaldiran in 1524 and was succeeded by his son Tahmasb.

AFTER ISMAʻIL

During the years between Shah Ismaʻil's death and Shah ʻAbbas's accession, the Safavid empire had to cope with a number of problems. In military terms, they had to engage in warfare on two frontiers in an attempt to preserve what Ismaʻil had won. On the western front their enemy was the Ottomans, galvanized and emboldened by their victory at Chaldiran, and now led by the famous sultan Suleyman "the Magnificent." Assisted by Qizilbash defectors and the betrayal of Shah Tahmasb's brother, the Ottomans succeeded in taking Baghdad and Arab Iraq from the Safavids, as well as Kurdestan, and at one point even occupied Tabriz. The Ottoman threat to Tabriz caused the Safavids to move their capital to the city of Qazvin, almost 300 miles southeast of Tabriz. In the east the Safavids were confronted with the Uzbeks, a Turkic people led by a dynasty descended from Genghis Khan. The Uzbeks repeatedly attacked Khurasan and eventually succeeded in taking Herat – the center of culture and the arts in the Timurid period – and other key cities. The empire over which Shah ʻAbbas was to preside was no longer as large as Shah Ismaʻil's.

Politically, the main problem for the Safavids was their relationship with the people they had conquered. They had to devise ways in which they could cooperate with local power holders – after all, they could not simply kill off the entire population they sought to rule. The two main segments of the population were the Turkomans and the Iranians. While there were always exceptions to the rule, traditionally the Iranians filled the bureaucratic ranks and the Turkomans the military ranks. The Persian-speaking bureaucrats, the Tajiks, had been administrators for the numerous dynasties that had ruled Iran in the past, including the Mongols and the Timurids. They survived the political changes, often because the new invaders simply did not bring with them enough people to replace them. This was particularly true during the period of Mongol rule. When the Safavids came to power, this practice continued, and the Iranian populations ran the state bureaucracy. However, Ismaʻil also recruited large land-owning Iranian elites into positions traditionally reserved for "men of the sword." This policy, which certainly favored the Iranians, backfired upon his death, when the Qizilbash took advantage of the new king Shah Tahmasb, aged only ten at the time, to attempt to regain their power. They were successful to some extent, but were plagued by in-fighting which eventually spiraled into war.

QIZILBASH CULTURE AND SOCIETY

The Qizilbash, who had brought Shah Isma'il to the throne, held considerable prestige in early Safavid society. They were organized into *uymaqs* or tribes, each of which was headed by a khan. As adherents to the original Safaviyya Sufi order, they regarded each other as fellow disciples and spiritual equals. Some of the early important positions that the Qizilbash held indicate that they enjoyed both spiritual and political authority. One of these was the *divan begi*, who adjudicated matters of common law; another was the *khalifat al-khulafa*, who served as chief spiritual deputy in the domain, appointed deputies of the king (*khalifa*) in the provinces, and governed Baghdad after the Qizilbash took the city. A third was the *lala*, or tutor to the royal princes. The prestige of the *lala*, however, declined after Shah 'Abbas came to power, as the new monarch sought to assert his authority, as we shall discuss in greater detail below.

Some early travelers to the Safavid court recorded their impressions of Qizilbash society, and this gives us at least a glimpse into the Qizilbash universe. Michele Membré, an Italian ambassador who traveled to Tabriz during the reign of Shah Tahmasb, provides lively descriptions of Qizilbash society and certain unique and distinct Qizilbash rituals and ceremonies. Membré states that the Qizilbash were eager to speak with him, welcoming him into their homes for sometimes up to twenty days at a time, and were curious about and interested in events taking place in Europe. He saw

Qizilbash women, and described them as anything but submissive and secluded, retaining a certain amount of economic power and wealth, at least within the household:

> Their wives are very beautiful and wear beautiful, big, round pearls at their necks. These ladies are very agreeable and keep all their husbands' money. So the said Qizilbash love their wives a great deal. The ladies ride through the town like men and go with maids instead of grooms; and they go with the face covered with a white kerchief, so only the eyes are seen.
>
> (Membré, *Mission*, 31)

Membré also attended a Qizilbash wedding, where he heard guests participate in an hour of *dhikr*, a Sufi practice in which a particular phrase is repeatedly chanted for devotional purposes. At the same event, wedding guests also sang anti-Ottoman songs and songs composed by Shah Isma'il and Shah Tahmasb, took turns making financial contributions, danced, and shared a meal. Between the donations and the anti-Ottoman songs, the attendees took part in a unique ceremony of ritual beating for the *qurchis*, or royal guards. The *qurchis* were each beaten in turn on the behind with the stick of the Sufi path (*chub-i tariq*) by the spiritual leader (*khalifa*) as an expression of love for the king. Various forms of ritual beating ceremonies continued into the later Safavid period, transformed somewhat from the time of Shah Tahmasb into practices either undertaken as part of an initiation ceremony of sorts for induction into a specific department, or as part of the punishment and then absolution of one's sins.

IMPOSING SHI'ISM

Following Shah Isma'il's proclamation of Shi'ism as the religion of the land, the Safavids also had to find a way to make the policy stick. After all, the majority of the population was Sunni. This was perhaps the biggest problem of all for the Safavid rulers, for no one really seemed to know what Twelver Shi'ism was about. Although there were Shi'i enclaves in Iran in places such as Mashhad and Qum, the Safavids had to bring in clerics from outside to educate the general population. These clerics largely came from the Jabal 'Amil region of southern Syria (present-day southern Lebanon), still a Shi'i enclave today. They were installed in mosques to act as prayer leaders and religious authorities. Together with clerics from traditional Shi'i centers in Iran, they gradually established themselves as part of a religious class. Shah Isma'il's successor, Shah Tahmasb, tried to eradicate any lingering expressions of *ghuluww* religiosity. He also persecuted Sunnis, executing many and causing many others to go underground or leave for neighboring Mughal India. He comes across as a somewhat dour and stern figure in comparison with his predecessor, though he did write poetry, practice calligraphy, and pen his memoirs. He also issued a series of ordinances promoting strict morality, by banning alcohol, singing, and dancing.

The Safavid imposition of Shi'ism as the state religion did not proceed in a seamless, straightforward fashion. In the years before Shah 'Abbas became king, there had been tensions between clerics and the king, and within the rank of clerics themselves. Shah Tahmasb's successor, Isma'il II, even attempted to restore Iran to Sunnism, but about a year later, a group of Qizilbash, assisted by his sister, poisoned him to death, so he could not effect any permanent change. In general, however, the clerics gradually developed into a separate social group that supported the authority of the Safavid kings yet at the same time preserved a certain amount of autonomy for themselves. Overall, Shi'ism had become a state-run operation.

EARLY NOTIONS OF LEGITIMACY, POWER, AND AUTHORITY

One of the most crucial issues that monarchs throughout the Islamic world had to address was the question of legitimacy. In other words, what gave a particular individual the right to rule? The Mongol sacking of Baghdad in 1258 brought an end to the Islamic ruling institution of the caliphate. By that time, the institution itself had become greatly weakened, and the individuals who called themselves caliphs, or successors to the Prophet Muhammad, claimed religious authority but held very little political power beyond the borders of the city of Baghdad. In previous centuries, dynastic caliphs ruled over vast empires stretching from North Africa to Central Asia, but by approximately 950, warlords, kings, sultans, and other types of rulers had carved territory for themselves out of that larger empire. After 1258, Muslim rulers had to address, either directly or indirectly, the fact that there was no longer a single figure who claimed universal religious authority over the world's Muslims. In the absence of the caliphate, therefore, considerable political experimentation took place, with monarchs often invoking several different notions of authority.

In the early Safavid era, Isma'il and his immediate successors promoted their kingship in three general ways: first, by upholding the idea that the Safavid king was the head of the Safavid Sufi order. In this way, they made use of the family's past, extending their position as Sufi leaders to all of Iran rather than having just a local following. Second, they or their chroniclers referred to themselves as the "shadow of God on earth," a phrase that we see in medieval treatises on Persian kingship. The concept itself has close parallels with and draws on pre-Islamic Sasanian ideas of kingship in which the king was seen as the representative of God on earth. The concept of the king as the shadow of God was supported by a third element of Safavid legitimacy, in which Safavid kings claimed to be the representative of the Hidden Imam. The Hidden or Twelfth Imam was the twelfth Shi'i descendant of the Prophet Muhammad through the line of 'Ali and his sons Hasan and Husayn. He was popularly thought to have disappeared down a well, only to return at some future date to fill the world with justice. While in principle the Hidden Imam did not have any representative at all – as all communication between him and his followers had been cut off with the so-called "greater occultation" in approximately 941 – Shah Isma'il made such claims and more for himself, as we saw in his *ghuluww*-oriented poetry when he stated, for example, "My mother is Fatima, my father is 'Ali; and therefore I am the Pir of the Twelve Imams" (Minorsky, "Poetry," 1042a). This was an unprecedented and major deviation from the accepted Shi'i doctrine, which did not allow for individuals to make such elevated claims.

When Shah Tahmasb came to power, he rejected the *ghuluww* sentiments of his father, and in doing so he also rejected the possibility of his fulfilling the Hidden Imam's functions, at least in terms of the practice of jurisprudence and the pronouncement of authoritative doctrine. Instead, he relegated such responsibilities to the influential al-Karaki, the Shi'i scholar from Lebanon who first visited Iran at Shah Isma'il's request. Al-Karaki subsequently became the foremost religious official in Iran under Shah Tahmasb as the jurist of the age (*mujtahid al-zaman*) and the vicegerent of the Imam (*na'ib al-imam*).

Al-Karaki and certain later jurists argued in their writings that some functions of the Hidden Imam, namely those related to activities such as legal decisions and leading the congregational prayer, could be carried out by the Shi'i jurists, who were to exercise religious authority under the rubric of the "general vicegerency" (*niyaba 'amma*) of the Hidden Imam. Thus a distinction began to be made between the political and religious spheres, although none of this was very clearly spelled out, nor was there definitive consensus among all of the jurists on the matter. This left space for Safavid kings to continue their claim to authority, not the religious authority that had been delegated to the jurists, but political authority in ruling on behalf of the Hidden Imam as his vicegerent or representative. They made this claim primarily on the basis of their genealogy.

The Safavids placed great emphasis on their family tree that indicated they were physical descendants of Musa al-Kazim, the Seventh of the Twelve Imams that Shi'i Muslims venerate. Since the time of Shah Isma'il, nearly every Safavid chronicler included a copy of the Safavid genealogy in his history. Whereas the earliest versions of the Safavid genealogy did not trace the family back to Musa al-Kazim, by the time of Shah Isma'il, the family genealogy had been "expanded" to include him, and by Shah 'Abbas's time, it had become widely accepted as the only version of the Safavid genealogy. Said Arjomand cites as an example of this sort of legitimation the following passage from a chronicle written during the reign of Shah Tahmasb:

> The office of the Sovereignty of the world after the Prophet is reserved for the Commander of the Faithful ['Ali], and after Him, this exalted office belongs to the Twelve Imams; and anyone else who interferes in this matter is a tyrant (*ja'ir*). As the Ruler of the Age (*sultan-e zaman*) [and] the Lord of Command (*sahib-e amr*) ... is absent, it is right and necessary that a person from the exalted dynasty of 'Ali and Fatima, who is competent for this task, should give currency to the Commandment[s] of the Imam of the Age among God's worshippers.
>
> (Arjomand, *Shadow*, 181–182; Shirazi, *Takmilat*, 33–34)

Here, the chronicler confirms the notion held by Shi' jurists that in the absence of the Imam, any ruler is illegitimate, or a tyrant (*ja'ir*), but he then goes on to state that in this situation, the person most suited to rule should be a descendant of 'Ali.

IRAN AND THE WORLD: A BRIEF OVERVIEW

On the eve of Shah 'Abbas's becoming king, the Safavids were situated between two powerful empires. To the west, in Anatolia, the Arab lands, and eastern Europe, lay the Ottoman empire. The Ottomans, ruling from Istanbul, the former Byzantine capital Constantinople, challenged the Safavids not just militarily, but also ideologically: theirs was a multi-ethnic Sunni state whose emperors increasingly sought to distinguish themselves from their Shi'i Safavid neighbors. The Ottomans attached great prestige to having been the first Muslim rulers to conquer Constantinople and to their role as protectors of the twin holy cities of Mecca and Medina, as they safeguarded the pilgrimage for the faithful. To the east of the Safavids in Central Asia were the Uzbeks, who were descendants of Genghis Khan. The Uzbeks repeatedly challenged the Safavids for control of Khurasan. The Mughals, ruling southeast of the Safavids in India, promoted their right to rule as descendants of Timur, or Tamerlane. They were wealthy and powerful, and had fairly consistent diplomatic relations with the Safavids. The main area of contention between the Mughals and the Safavids was Qandahar, which changed hands several times during the course of the Safavid dynasty. Beyond the borders of these neighboring Islamic empires, the Safavids became involved in European affairs, as mercantile powers and trading companies – the Portuguese, the Dutch, and the English – were establishing commercial networks and trading posts in the Indian Ocean, and were becoming increasingly interested in trading with the Safavids.

This was the world into which Shah 'Abbas was born. Throughout his life as Safavid king, he sought to put Iran on this world stage. He used every means at his disposal to do so, and was remarkably successful. However, he grew up in tumultuous times and barely managed to become king at all.

2

EARLY YEARS: 1571–1598

THE IMMEDIATE CONTEXT: THE REIGNS OF SHAH ISMA'IL II AND MUHAMMAD KHUDABANDA

'Abbas was only five years old when his grandfather, Shah Tahmasb, died in 1576. Shah Tahmasb was succeeded by his sons, Isma'il II (r. 1576–1577) and Muhammad Khudabanda (r. 1578–1587), 'Abbas's father. Isma'il II goes down in history primarily for his attempt to revert Iran back to Sunni Islam, an experiment that utterly failed. He also endeavored to re-impose order in Iran in a harsh fashion, as bandits and Turkoman raids had killed thousands of people. Consequently, he had Qizilbash officers executed, along with anyone else whom he perceived to be a threat to his rule. Because of this, a group of Qizilbash, assisted by his sister, Pari Khan Khanum, poisoned his habitual dose of opium and killed him. Isma'il II was succeeded by his oldest brother, the nearly blind Muhammad Khudabanda, who was too weak to stop the ongoing contention between and among the Qizilbash tribes, with one faction in control of Qazvin and another in control of Khurasan.

In fact, during his first year as king, Muhammad Khudabanda was weak and ineffective, which provided the political space for his wife, Khayr al-Nisa Begum, known as Mahd-i 'Ulya, to step in and act, effectively, as ruler. Mahd-i 'Ulya was Shah 'Abbas's mother and a daughter of Mir 'Abd Allah Khan, the latest in a line of Mar'ashi sayyids (descendants of the Prophet Muhammad) who ruled

Mazandaran. Mahd-i 'Ulya, having had Pari Khan Khanum killed in February 1578, ruled until 1579, when she herself was strangled to death by a group of Qizilbash who resented her position.

THE BIRTH OF SHAH 'ABBAS

> When 'Abbas Mirza was born at Herat, signs of his great destiny were visible upon his brow.
>
> (*TAA*, 128/210)

This is how Iskandar Beg Munshi, official chronicler to Shah 'Abbas, begins the account of 'Abbas's birth. Unsurprisingly, all of Shah 'Abbas's chroniclers narrate this event as a great occasion laden with cosmological signs of his divine destiny to rule. Iskandar Beg goes on to establish a special connection between the newborn prince and his grandfather, Shah Tahmasb, whose reign had lasted more than fifty years (from 1524 to 1576). Shah Tahmasb, he says, would send a carpet and a cradle to every new-born boy in the royal family, but what he sent to 'Abbas was no ordinary carpet; rather, it was one which had originally been "spread beneath his own royal throne in the Chehel Sotun hall of the palace at Qazvin" (*TAA*, 129/210). Clearly, Shah Tahmasb foresaw that of all the many children in the royal family, this was a child that would be king. In another episode, 'Abbas's father sent Shah Tahmasb the news of the birth of his son, asking him to give him a name. At that time, Shah Tahmasb just happened to be writing a poem that had the name 'Abbas in it, and so this was the name he chose. Another of Shah 'Abbas's chroniclers, his royal astrologer Munajjim Yazdi, opens his history with a description of the astrological phenomena associated with the birth of the king and notes the auspicious nature of the stars and zodiac constellations at that time. From these accounts, we are left in no doubt that 'Abbas was destined to be a great king from the very start.

Actually, it was far from obvious that 'Abbas was going to become king at all. He was born on 27 January 1571 in the eastern Iranian city of Herat, in modern-day Afghanistan, as the third offspring of Muhammad Khudabanda. When ʻAbbas was six years old, his uncle Ismaʻil II succeeded Shah Tahmasb. One of the first things Ismaʻil II did as the new king was to have his own brothers executed (Abbas's father survived, though blinded) along with anyone else whom he believed a threat to his rule, including ʻAbbas's tutor/guardian (*lala*). Whether he did this out of desire to emulate a practice current under the Ottomans, or as a result of long years of imprisonment and drug use, is unclear.

ʻAbbas's *lala* was not a tutor in the ordinary sense of the word. Rather, the *lala* played a significant role in the Safavid dynasty. The Safavids had inherited from the earlier Turkoman dynasties the practice in which royal princes were tutored by an individual – a *lala* – who held a prominent position in the Safavid state. For example, Shah Tahmasb's tutor was from the Rumlu Qizilbash tribe, and he also held the position of *amir al-umara*, or "great amir." These *lalas* could become too influential for the king's liking or become involved in succession politics – Shah Tahmasb, for example, shot his *lala* to death with an arrow after he tried to wield too much power. Without a powerful *lala*, the young ʻAbbas ("ʻAbbas Mirza," or "Prince ʻAbbas," as he was called) had no chance of succeeding to the throne.

After executing ʻAbbas's *lala*, Ismaʻil II then appointed a Qizilbash named ʻAli Quli Khan of the Shamlu tribe as governor of Herat, giving him secret orders to execute the young prince. But ʻAli Quli Khan was reluctant to carry out the orders and Ismaʻil II himself was murdered after ruling for only about a year, as described in chapter 1, so ʻAbbas survived.

FIRST ATTEMPTS TO PLACE ʻABBAS MIRZA ON THE THRONE

Having avoided being murdered, ʻAbbas was then raised to the throne prematurely in 1581, when he was only ten years old. This was due to the scheming of the Qizilbash tribes, who used him to further their own political aspirations and vendettas while at the same time taking full advantage of the weakness and incompetence of the king, Muhammad Khudabanda. The young prince became indirectly involved in Qizilbash politics and was at the center of a rebellion in which Khurasan, the province where he was residing, attempted to break away from the central Safavid government. One of the key individuals involved in the rebellion – the above mentioned 'Ali Quli Khan, who had resisted orders to murder 'Abbas when Isma'il II was in power – had become the prince's tutor after his appointment to the governorship of Herat. Herat and Mashhad, the resting place of the Eighth Imam of the Twelver Shi'i, were the two most important cities in the province of Khurasan. 'Ali Quli Khan was involved in a struggle against the governor of Mashhad, a certain Murtaza Quli Khan. He defeated Murtaza Quli Khan, even after the latter received reinforcement troops from the central court. The nature of Qizilbash rivalries at this time was such that when a particular individual was defeated, the relatives of the victor would face reprisals. Thus, 'Ali Quli Khan's kinsmen at the court suffered the consequences of his victory against Murtaza Quli Khan.

In retaliation, 'Ali Quli Khan and his ally Murshid Quli Khan, an Ustajlu Qizilbash leader, along with a group of Qizilbash from their respective tribes, put the ten-year-old 'Abbas on the throne. Although the prince was not universally recognized as king, this was a genuine coronation, for they struck coins and read the Friday sermon in his name, two steps traditionally taken when a new king came to power, thereby indicating that he was now the sovereign. But while 'Abbas had the support of the Shamlu and Ustajlu Qizilbash, two other Qizilbash tribes, the Turkoman and Takkalu, held sway over his father, Muhammad Khudabanda. Other Qizilbash factions had supported three of 'Abbas's brothers (the princes Tahmasb, Hamza, and Abu Talib). It was the backers of Muhammad Khudabanda who won, and soon thereafter, Muhammad Khudabanda and his army marched on Herat, forcing 'Ali Quli Khan, the "king maker," to surrender, thus ending 'Abbas's first bid for the throne. 'Abbas Mirza remained in Khurasan, however, with Murshid Quli Khan the Ustajlu now acting as his deputy and guardian. This episode reflects the weakness of Muhammad Khudabanda and indicates the degree to which he lacked control over his own kingdom – a situation that 'Abbas would inherit once he officially succeeded his father.

'ABBAS MIRZA'S SECOND ENTHRONEMENT

'Abbas had better luck the second time around. When Hamza Mirza, 'Abbas's older brother and primary contender for the throne, who had wielded considerable power after 1581, was assassinated on 6 December 1586, possibly at the instigation of some of his own men, the way was clear for a second attempt to place 'Abbas on the throne. This time, Murshid Quli Khan kidnapped the young prince and took him to the eastern Iranian city of Mashhad, presumably to protect him from being killed. Murshid Quli Khan had recently been made governor of the city and used Mashhad as a base to gain support for 'Abbas in Khurasan and elsewhere in Iran. In 1588, he marched on Qazvin, the capital city, and had 'Abbas enthroned, effectively forcing out his father, Shah Muhammad Khudabanda. Shah 'Abbas was sixteen years old at the time and was now the new Safavid king.

After his coronation, Shah 'Abbas received various family members who had come to Qazvin to show their support. The next day, he gathered together an assembly of generals (amirs), Qizilbash, and other high-ranking state officials. They acknowledged him as their monarch and pledged their loyalty to him. For all that, he immediately had those responsible for the murder of his brother, Hamza Mirza, executed.

SHAH 'ABBAS IN POWER

> He [Shah 'Abbas] was confronted by two powerful monarchs, the problem of Qizilbash disunity had not been solved, and he was faced by domestic revolts … and by rebellions on the part of the

> semi-independent rulers on the borders of the Safavid empire, who had taken advantage of fifteen years of weak Safavid rule since the death of Shah Tahmasb to shake off Safavid suzerainty and assert their independence.
>
> (*TAA*, 409–410/587)

In this succinct passage, Iskandar Beg clearly describes the problems that Shah 'Abbas faced upon becoming king during this first phase, when the Safavid capital was still in the city of Qazvin (from 1587 to 1598). The first and most serious threat was the internal one: the Qizilbash who had put him on the throne, though somewhat weakened as a result of having entered a period of internal conflict and strife, remained intent on preserving their position. This was the second time since the Safavids came to power that the Qizilbash experienced conflict of such intensity among themselves; the first was from 1524 to 1536, during the initial decade of Shah Tahmasb's reign. Despite Shah 'Abbas's immediate purging of their ranks after he came to the throne, they still posed a challenge to his authority. Many were powerful governors of important cities and provinces of Iran, and in some cases they boldly ruled these areas in an almost independent fashion. His initial task, upon which the remainder of his career as king rested, was to re-conquer Iran.

SHAH 'ABBAS AND THE QIZILBASH

Shah 'Abbas's overall approach to curbing Qizilbash power was to raise a new army consisting of *ghulam*s who had been purchased as slaves from the Caucasus and initially brought into Iran during the reign of Shah Tahmasb. However, the process through which the *ghulam*s (who will be discussed more fully later) were transformed into a new elite army was a gradual one, which meant that the king had to deal with the Qizilbash threat before the *ghulam* army became fully effective. This he accomplished through a persistent effort to eliminate those Qizilbash leaders who challenged his power and gradually replace them with *ghulam*s.

Shah 'Abbas began the process by executing a group of Qizilbash who were conspiring to kill Murshid Quli Khan, the Ustajlu who had put him on the throne. Later, upon learning that Murshid Quli Khan had plans to kill him, he had him executed too, in the summer of 1589. These events, occurring so soon after he came to power, gave him the determination to continue removing, one by one, those who posed a threat to his rule.

A number of important Qizilbash rulers lost their lives as a result of this campaign. These included (1) Bektash Khan, the Afshar Qizilbash who had been in control of Fars (where the city of Shiraz is located), Kirman, and Yazd, (2) Ya'qub Khan, the Dhu'l Qadr who then assumed control over those areas, and (3) Farhad Khan Qaramanlu, an important general and trusted advisor to the king, whose story will be told in chapter 5, below.

Bektash Khan and Ya'qub Khan were local governors who were killed due to their arrogance, their unwillingness to present themselves to the king at the court, and their greed. Bektash Khan was the Afshar who ruled over Kirman and Yazd, and Ya'qub Khan the Dhu'l Qadr who was in control of Fars. These two ambitious men, with designs on territory beyond the limits of their royal appointments, and their followers were fighting against each other. When Bektash Khan rebelled against Shah 'Abbas, the king ordered Ya'qub Khan to subdue him. Ya'qub Khan's men eventually killed Bektash Khan in 1589–1590 and Ya'qub Khan sent his head to the court. In doing this, Ya'qub Khan expressed loyalty and obedience to the king.

The Dhu'l Qadr victory over the Afshars did not last for long, however, as Ya'qub Khan's defiance of the king and independent actions led to his own downfall. A number of sources tell the story of the king and the khan, and they portray the conflict as one between a greedy, proud, and defiant Qizilbash leader and an intelligent, patient king. For Shah 'Abbas's chroniclers, this was epic-worthy high drama par excellence. Several of them provided detailed descriptions of Ya'qub Khan's defeat, and one chronicler went so far as to say that the story of Yaqub Khan was *the* deciding factor that inspired him to write his history:

> When the news of this manifest victory spread far and wide throughout Iran, it became a source of astonishment to the masters of knowledge because the fortress of Istakhr, by virtue of its strength, had been a source of glory to the Eastern kings ... The strangeness of this wonderful incident and the good fortune of the 'Alid king became the reason for the limping pen to hasten in writing this story.
> (Natanzi, *Naqavat*, 7–8)

After his defeat of Bektash Khan, Ya'qub Khan took control of his former territory and thus held Fars, Kirman, Abarquh, and Yazd. However, he had executed nearly twenty Dhu'l Qadrs who threatened his position as governor of Shiraz. When Shah 'Abbas found out about Ya'qub Khan's behavior, he headed for Fars in order to deal with him. As part of an elaborate cat and mouse game, Ya'qub Khan, knowing that the king's army would come after him, entered the famed pre-Islamic fortress of Istakhr. After considerable diplomacy, Shah 'Abbas persuaded the khan to leave the fortress and proceed towards Shiraz. There, he was executed along with a number of his followers. The king appointed a prominent *ghulam* to take the khan's place. This brought the internal warfare of the Qizilbash to an end.

The account of Shah 'Abbas and Ya'qub Khan was not just a solitary contest between the shrewd, diplomatic, and generously patient monarch and the cowardly, arrogant khan who paid no heed to the king's warnings, as the chroniclers would lead us to believe. The larger contexts include Shah 'Abbas's need for manpower to fight in the military operation he was planning against the Uzbeks, and his desire to control the southern portion of Iran in order ultimately to gain control over the Persian Gulf. Thus, the steps he took to establish his authority in Iran had ramifications on the world scene, and are a reflection of his ability to understand the global impact of local events and situations, and shape them to his advantage. Ya'qub Khan was eventually replaced by the eminent *ghulam* Allahverdi Khan, who would later lead Shah 'Abbas's troops in the Khurasan campaign and take part in the construction of Isfahan, as we shall discuss below.

While he was able to curb Qizilbash political power, Shah 'Abbas had less success in putting an end to Qizilbash cultural practices such as the *chiragh-kushan*. In his memoirs, Shah Tahmasb spoke disapprovingly of a ritual known as *chiragh-kushan*, in which a group of men and women "engaged in a promiscuous and indiscriminate orgy," once the lights were extinguished (Morton, "Chub-i Tariq," 239–240). This practice was associated not only with the Qizilbash, but also Isma'ilis and Ahl-i Haqq groups. It appears to have survived into the Shah 'Abbas period, for the German traveler Adam Olearius, writing in 1638, relates a story in which Shah 'Abbas found out about an instance of *chiragh-kushan* taking place in a village, and "ordered all of the Inhabitants of the Village, to be cut to pieces, without any regard or distinction of age or sex, and peopled it with others" (Morton, "Chub-i Tariq," 240). Further evidence indicating that Shah 'Abbas tried to put an end to the activities described here can be found in an appointment deed document (*shajara*). Such documents named new deputies (*khalifas*) initiated into the Safaviyya Sufi order and gave them instructions on how their disciples should behave. In one such *shajara* document, Shah 'Abbas orders the disciples not to associate with "strange women." A. H. Morton believes that this directive is aimed at previous Qizilbash customs that were no longer deemed appropriate during Shah 'Abbas's time (Morton, "Chub-i Tariq," 241–242). Nevertheless, read "against the grain," the fact that the appointment deed contained this particular order suggests the longevity of such Qizilbash cultural practices.

EXTERNAL CHALLENGES: THE OTTOMAN TRUCE

Despite his successes against the Qizilbash, it took some time until Shah 'Abbas was fully ready to deal with the external threats to the Safavid empire. Before enjoying any military victory, he suffered two humiliating losses, one against the Ottomans and the other against the Mughals. In the case of the Ottomans, he was forced to sign a peace treaty, the Peace of Istanbul, on 21 March 1590, just a few months before Ya'qub Khan left the fortress of Istakhr. Earlier, in 1578, under their ruler Sultan Murad, the Ottomans had invaded Azerbaijan, and the Safavids had suffered a number of losses. This treaty allowed the Ottomans to annex that territory they had occupied in "Azerbayjan, Qarabagh, Ganja, Qarajadagh, Georgia, and parts of Luristan and Kurdistan." Shah 'Abbas signed it to avoid fighting against the Ottomans and the Uzbeks at the same time. Iskandar Beg acknowledges how humiliating this was for the king, stating that the terms of this treaty were "repugnant both to the Shah and the army" (*TAA*, 410/587). Another chronicler, known as "Don Juan," was an Iranian who went to Spain and converted to Catholicism. Don Juan notes two other similarly humiliating stipulations in this treaty. One was that Shah 'Abbas had to send to the Ottoman Sultan Murad in Istanbul his nephew Sultan Haydar Mirza as hostage, and he had to promise that he would stop the practice of publicly cursing the first three successors to the Prophet Muhammad, seen by Shi'i Muslims as illegitimate usurpers of the position which was rightfully 'Ali's.

EXTERNAL CHALLENGES: RELATIONS WITH THE MUGHALS

Shah 'Abbas also suffered a defeat against the Mughals. The biggest point of contention here was Qandahar, which the Safavids had held since the time of Shah Tahmasb. However, a few years after the Ottoman peace treaty, in 1594, the Mughals marched into the city of Qandahar and took over its fortress. The Mughal empire at the time was ruled by the emperor Akbar, a unique monarch who was engaged in his own religious experiments that included the creation of a new syncretic religion with himself at its center.

In general, Safavid relations with the Mughals were better than with any other neighboring empire or ruling dynasty. This was, perhaps, partly because Humayun (r. 1539–1544), the second emperor of the Mughal dynasty and son of its founder, Babur (r. 1526–1530), had to take refuge in Iran during the reign of Shah

Tahmasb while fleeing from his enemies. Tahmasb played this to his political advantage, turning Humayun's visit into a propaganda tour de force. He took Humayun on a well-publicized tour of the Safavid ancestral home in Ardabil, had him participate in other high-visibility events, and even made him sign a document stating that he had converted to Shi'ism, which must have been extremely embarrassing for the emperor, however much he repudiated the "conversion" upon his return to India. Thereafter the Safavid chroniclers emphasized the positive relations between the two dynasties, and Safavid kings continued to take advantage of the memory of Humayun's visit, for example by depicting the meeting between him and Shah Tahmasb on a huge mural in the Chihil Sutun palace in Isfahan.

At the time of Shah 'Abbas's accession, Qandahar was governed by a prince of the Safavid house: Muzaffar Husayn Mirza, whose brother, Rustam Mirza, controlled Garmsirat and Zamin Davar. These two princes were sons of Sultan Husayn Mirza, a nephew of Shah Tahmasb. Sultan Husayn Mirza was appointed governor of Qandahar when Shah Tahmasb was in power, and when he died, during the reign of Isma'il II, his son Muzaffar Husayn Mirza took over. The two brothers, who often fought each other for territory, knew that the Mughal emperor Akbar had designs on Qandahar. They also recognized that the Uzbeks were in a position to seize the city. The Uzbek threat, then, probably inspired Rustam Mirza to abandon Qandahar, go to India, and enter the service of the Mughals. Upon arriving there, he received the governorship of Sambal and command over 5000 troops. His brother followed shortly thereafter.

This was neither the first nor the last example of prominent Safavids leaving Safavid territory for the Mughal empire, where both the job opportunities and the pay were better than in Iran. Indeed, a stream of poets, chroniclers, and others, some fleeing religious persecution at the hands of the Safavids, went to India, where they prospered both intellectually and materially. At any rate, the brothers' defection made it possible for the Mughals to take Qandahar, which they did in 1595. Although Shah 'Abbas could not have been very pleased with this turn of events, as in the case of the Ottoman peace treaty, he was simply not strong enough to do anything about it until the situation within Iran improved. Qandahar remained in Mughal hands until Shah 'Abbas recaptured it towards the end of his reign in 1622, as will be discussed in chapter 7.

GILAN AND MAZANDARAN

While Shah 'Abbas had to postpone dealing with the Ottomans and lost territory to the Mughals, he had greater success closer to home in his campaigns to Gilan and Mazandaran. As provinces situated near the Caspian Sea, Gilan and Mazandaran were two important regions for silk cultivation and agricultural production. During this time, Gilan was governed by Khan Ahmad Khan, a local ruler and Shah 'Abbas's brother-in-law (he was married to the king's sister). Khan Ahmad Khan had criticized Shah 'Abbas for entering a peace treaty with the Ottomans, and was planning a joint attack with the Ottomans against the Safavid king. As for Mazandaran, it was all but independently ruled by Mar'ashi sayyids. Shah 'Abbas dispatched his general, Farhad Khan Qaramanlu, to subdue both regions, which he accomplished by 1596. As a result, the area not only came under Shah 'Abbas's direct control, but it also brought him increased revenue, as he converted it to crown land.

THE NEW *GHULAM* ARMY

While Farhad Khan Qaramanlu was able to remain in the Shah's favor until the Uzbek campaign of 1598, the death of Ya'qub Khan Dhu'l Qadr marked the end of Qizilbash supremacy in the Safavid military. In approximately 1590, Shah 'Abbas established a new corps of soldiers, known as the *ghulaman-i khassa-yi sharifa*, or "crown servants," drawn from the Caucasus region (Georgia, Armenia, and Circassia), to form the main backbone of his army and to act as a counter-weight to the Qizilbash. The first captives from the Caucasus, mostly Christian women and children captured during or after battle, had already been brought to Iran at the time of Shah Tahmasb. As will be discussed in greater detail in chapter 3, after moving the capital, Shah 'Abbas himself orchestrated the forced transfer and movement of large populations from the Caucasus as part of his project to consolidate and centralize his rule and to expand the Safavid royal household. But even before this, Shah 'Abbas used the Georgians for political gain. Early on in his reign, he appointed a royal *ghulam* as *darugha* or mayor of the city of Isfahan and a Georgian prince as mayor of Qazvin, his capital city at the time. His motives for doing this formed part of his plan to build a pro-Georgian faction at the court to help him recover the territories in the Caucasus that had been lost to the Ottomans.

Over time, the *ghulam*s and their descendants, nominally converted to Islam, became an important element in Safavid society. Some entered the royal harem and became wives of the Safavid kings, often involving themselves in contentious succession politics in order to ensure that their sons would become king. Others served in the royal household and became part of the Safavid administration. Still others trained together in separate quarters and became part of the king's new army. Raising an army made up of *ghulam*s was a deliberate policy decision on the part of the king and was in a sense the culmination of practices that had been developing earlier on. In order to divide the Qizilbash tribes, Shah 'Abbas would show favor to individual tribal leaders in exchange for their complete loyalty and "love for the king" (*shahsevan*). The king eventually extended this practice to the *ghulam*s as well, but he did not have to compete with a tribal leader as he did with the Qizilbash in order to gain their devotion.

Like their Ottoman counterparts, the janissaries, the Safavid *ghulam*s were for the most part loyal to the king throughout the rest of the Safavid period. As the Qizilbash continued to lose power, the new *ghulam* corps changed the balance of power in Safavid society and formed a new elite class in Iran. The Safavids did not consistently engage in military raids for fresh recruits in every generation, unlike some other Islamic dynasties. Rather, *ghulam* descendants could and did hold high positions in the government and military. They also became important patrons of the arts and involved themselves in the economic life of the dynasty.

To command his new army, Shah 'Abbas appointed the Georgian *ghulam* Allahverdi Khan, whom he had already named as Ya'qub Khan's replacement. Allahverdi Khan's rise to power was quick, and shows how effectively Shah 'Abbas's reforms were progressing. In addition to serving as commander of the *ghulam* forces, Allahverdi Khan also became governor-general (*beglerbegi*) of Fars and Kuhgiluyah after the death of Ya'qub Khan. Allahverdi Khan was the first *ghulam* to receive governorships previously held only by the Qizilbash. He married a Georgian woman – as did other notable Georgian *ghulams* at this time – and his entire family achieved high positions, with his sons eventually enjoying prestigious careers in the Safavid state.

On the whole, Shah 'Abbas succeeded in curbing Qizilbash supremacy. It is important to note here that this did not mean the Qizilbash faded entirely from the scene, nor were they completely marginalized or eliminated, as they continued to play an important role in the Safavid state. This says a great deal about Shah 'Abbas's ability to avoid alienating various constituencies of his empire. Indeed, as Andrew Newman has pointed out, "non-*ghulam* elements," including the Qizilbash, continued to be important and fought alongside the *ghulams*, and they continued to hold positions of prominence as provincial governors (Newman, *Safavid*, 53–54).

SHAH 'ABBAS AND THE SUFI ORDERS

This early phase of Shah 'Abbas's rule was one of transition in terms of his attitudes towards religion. By the time he took the throne, some of the initial religious impulses of the Safavids, such as Sufism and *ghuluww* religiosity, had started to fade, yet traces were still apparent. As a new king, Shah ʻAbbas initially showed interest in unorthodox religious movements, only later to suppress them.

Shah ʻAbbas's predecessors had already begun to clamp down on popular Sufi orders in Iran. Even though the Safavids themselves originated as a Sufi order, after 1501, when Shiʻism was established as the religion of the land, potential and actual rivals, including Sufi orders, were persecuted and/or driven to exile, in particular those that professed Sunnism. Some of the most prominent groups, such as the Naqshbandiyya, the Khalvatiyya, and the Nurbakhshiyya, did not survive through the Safavid period as organized orders. Others, such as the Niʻmatallahiyya, survived but in a very different form. One of the Christian Carmelites who visited Iran during the reign of Shah ʻAbbas described the traditional ascetic lifestyle of the Sufis, and then explained how their status had declined by the time he arrived in 1604:

> Nowadays there are hardly any of them who observe that mode of life and, although they may do so outwardly to some extent, in the matter of poverty in particular, they are very sensual and marry, receive money, drink wine, do not observe the fasts, and have many other vices, for which reason the Shah does not esteem them, nor does any person of quality, but only the common people.
>
> (*Carmelites* I, 156)

Elsewhere we learn that Sufis held much lower positions under Shah ʻAbbas than they had in the past, such as palace sweeper.

The Niʻmatallahis, an important Sufi order founded by Shah Niʻmatallah Vali (d. 1431), provide an example of how Sufism and Sufi orders changed and evolved in the Safavid period, and how Shah ʻAbbas took advantage of such transformations and manipulated them to his benefit. Initially, the Niʻmatallahis followed Sunni Islam and ran into sectarian conflict with another Sufi order in Iran, the Shiʻi Haydariyya, founded around the same time as the Niʻmatallahis by Sultan Qutb al-Din Haydar (d. 1426–1427). Some time after the reign of Shah Ismaʻil, the Niʻmatallahis converted to Shiʻism and during Tahmasb's reign, a number of marriages between the Niʻmatallahi and Safavid families took place.

The relationship between the dynasty and the Sufi order was a good one until Shah 'Abbas's reign, when a Ni'matallahi became involved in a Qizilbash rebellion and thereafter the Ni'matallahis ceased to exist as a traditional Sufi order in Iran.

Ultimately, the Ni'matallahis only survived as what one scholar has termed a Nimati "gang" (*EI2*, "Nimat Allahiyya"). When the Ni'matallahis earlier clashed with the Haydariyya, the basis of the conflict was sectarian, or Sunni versus Shi'i, respectively. By Shah 'Abbas's reign, however, the Ni'matallahi conflict with the Haydariyya continued, but it was stripped of its sectarian nature and the orders lost their traditional Sufi identities. What remained instead was something approximating "neighborhood factional strife" of the type that the people of Ardabil were free of according to the *Safvat al-safa*. We hear much of the Nimati/Haydari fights that took place in Iranian cities such as Tabriz and Shiraz. Later travelers to Safavid Iran observe that nearly all cities in Iran were divided into quarters or wards associated with either the Nimatis or the Haydaris, as they were called at that time. Membership in one or other of these wards had nothing to do with Sufism as a belief system, or even any other sort of religious affiliation, and the fighting was not related to any other kind of particular association, whether political or social.

Shah 'Abbas displayed his ability to play off one rival party against another to his own advantage with the Nimati/Haydari factionalism, and even encouraged their aggressive behavior. The idea was that if large groups in urban areas showed antagonism towards each other, the likelihood of their demonstrating loyalty to the king would increase. The Italian traveler Pietro Della Valle (1586–1652) notes the king's role in the conflict:

> Shah 'Abbas sometimes intervenes to incite the two factions and, having brought them satisfactorily to blows, nimbly quits the field and sits at a window watching the ensuing battle and its dismal consequences.
>
> (quoted in Mirjafari, "Haydari," 147)

Although participants fought with sticks and stones, the fighting was intense enough for people to be killed. Shah 'Abbas's court astrologer and chronicler describes a battle between the two groups in Qazvin:

> on Sunday the 19th Rabi' I [1594–1595] we arrived at Qazvin, and on Tuesday the 20th Jumadi I there took place by royal decree a battle of the Ni'matis and Haydaris on the Maydan-i Sa'adat in Qazvin. Victory fell to the Mir Haydari party ... a similar fight was also decreed at the shrine of Shahzada Husayn.
>
> (quoted in Mirjafari, "Haydari," 147)

SUPPRESSION OF RELIGIOUS HERESIES: THE NUQTAVIS

While Shah 'Abbas turned the presence of Nimatis and Haydaris in Iran to his advantage, he could not tolerate the existence of certain other groups in any way whatsoever. One striking example of this is the Nuqtavi movement. Shah 'Abbas's suppression of the Nuqtavis represents the triumph of orthodox Shi'ism over religious heterodoxy and was accomplished during this phase of his reign. Initially, however, he showed considerable interest in this unusual religious faction that was viewed as a heresy. Nuqtavism, an offshoot of Hurufism – itself a fourteenth-century movement that connected humans with letters of the alphabet and their numerical values – was founded by Mahmud Pasikhani in the late fourteenth century. Like Shah Isma'il, Pasikhani laid claim to inaugurating a new religious "dispensation" and made messianic claims for himself. Among Nuqtavi beliefs, which the prolific Pasikhani set out in over 1000 treatises and sixteen books, is the notion that the four elements – earth, fire, water, and air – form the basis of creation and evolution. Everything, then, comes from these elements in different combinations, and particles of being formed from the four elements can move from one form of existence to another. Therefore, on this elemental level, humans are related to stars and planets and may undergo reincarnation. Pasikhani himself claimed to be a reincarnation of the Prophet Muhammad and Imam 'Ali. The Nuqtavis also shared certain ideas with other groups; for example, like some Sufis and *ghuluww* groups, they believed in a unity of existence and recognized a potential divinity in every person. During the time of Shah Isma'il, the Nuqtavis emerged as an important force in Iran and the movement spread to various cities in Iran, notably Qazvin.

When he was arrested in 1593, a Nuqtavi named Mir Sayyid Ahmad Kashi, author of books on Nuqtavism, had in his possession a treatise on Nuqtavi gnosis, and Iskandar Beg Munshi makes disparaging comments about the ideas contained in this book. These provide us with some sense of what the Safavids themselves considered heretical religious belief at the time of Shah 'Abbas. Iskandar Beg notes that among Kashi's beliefs was a rejection of the resurrection and the Day of Judgment, and the idea that heaven and hell should be understood in terms of the rewards and punishments received from one's actions in this world.

The key Nuqtavi figure with whom Shah 'Abbas interacted was Darvish Khusraw, a Nuqtavi who was active during the time of Shah Tahmasb. Darvish Khusraw came from a line of well and irrigation diggers. At some stage in his life, he left these professions and became a dervish, dressing in dervish clothing. He subsequently met some Nuqtavis and when he became acquainted with their teachings, he embraced their cause, started teaching Nuqtavism, and gained his own following of dervishes. After the death of Shah Tahmasb, he built a center for his followers, among whom were a number of Qizilbash, in Qazvin.

Darvish Khusraw was still active when Shah 'Abbas came to power. Shah 'Abbas learned about Nuqtavism from other individuals at the Sufi lodge associated with Darvish Khusraw and became close with the darvish after he started frequenting the center. Why he should have done so has been a topic of considerable debate. Maybe he simply wanted to keep an eye on their activities to ensure that they did not threaten his rule. Iskandar Beg claims that the king wanted to understand the dervish, and therefore adopted "the manner of speech used by travelers on the mystical way, and unfolded his own personal knowledge of God to him [Darvish Khusraw] after the fashion of dervishes" (*TAA*, 474/648). But Iskandar Beg could just be covering up what was a genuine interest in Nuqtavism on the part of the king; a seventeenth-century Indian source states that Shah 'Abbas was actually initiated into the Nuqtavi order. One scholar has suggested that this early inclination towards Nuqtavi belief could perhaps help explain his lack of interest in following religious laws later in his life, although he may have already had an inclination against adhering to formal religious strictures (*EI2*, "Nuktawiyya").

While we may never be sure of his motivation, Shah 'Abbas's relations with the Nuqtavis eventually took a turn for the worse. In 1591, he suppressed a Nuqtavi uprising in the Fars region. Two years later, Darvish Khusraw, still feeling he had the upper hand, arrogantly warned the king, who had gone to Luristan to put down a (non-Nuqtavi) rebellion in that region, that a Nuqtavi would replace him on the throne if he did not return to Qazvin by a particular date. Qazvin seemed poised for a full-fledged Nuqtavi uprising, and Darvish Khusraw seemed poised for a severe punishment from the king. Darvish Khusraw's downfall began when Shah 'Abbas returned from Luristan, summoned the darvish to his presence, and launched an investigation into his activities. Iskandar Beg explains that initially, Darvish Khusraw's Nuqtavi inclinations had not been fully apparent to the king. However, when a search of his center turned up wine vats, Shah 'Abbas considered this antinomianism as evidence of his still being a Nuqtavi and had him "tied by his throat to the saddle of a camel and dragged around the city" (*TAA*, 486/649). This execution was part of a larger campaign of suppression in which anybody that the king considered a Nuqtavi was killed. Among them were poets, artists, and philosophers and even those who served the king at the court. The learned Mir Sayyid Ahmad Kashi mentioned above was also killed at this time.

SHAH 'ABBAS'S TEMPORARY DETHRONEMENT

In the midst of and indeed as part of the Nuqtavi purges, one of the most intriguing events in Shah 'Abbas's career took place. It began when his royal astrologer foretold the death of a royal personage due to an inauspicious alignment of the planets Mars and Saturn soon to occur. How would they deal with this bad omen? Shah 'Abbas and the astrologer concocted a plan in which they would seat someone else in the king's place during the three dangerous days of the planetary conjunction, after which the "replacement king" would be executed. This would presumably keep the real king safe from any harm.

Shah 'Abbas chose a Nuqtavi, Ustad Yusufi the "quiver maker," as his stand-in, because, according to Iskandar Beg, his "heresy was more heinous than that of his fellows" (*TAA*, 474/648). Shah 'Abbas and Ustad Yusufi were already acquainted; Yusufi had made quivers for the king upon his request and had shared something of Nuqtavi beliefs with him. Ustad Yusufi was crowned and invested with full royal regalia in a ceremony that all the courtiers attended. Dressed in magnificent robes and seated upon a mule adorned with jewel-encrusted harnessing, he celebrated his new position with food and drink. Knowing fully well what fate awaited him, he made the most of his three days of playing king, and enjoyed threatening to execute the court astrologer who had made the original prediction. Meanwhile, Shah 'Abbas did not partake in any of his usual kingly activities and instead kept a low profile, staying with a few servants and grooms. When the three days were over, Shah 'Abbas returned and had Ustad Yusufi killed.

The Nuqtavi executions mark a turning point in Shah 'Abbas's career and in Iran's religious history, in particular its tradition of giving birth to *ghuluww* movements. Kathryn Babayan has commented on the significance of this episode, noting that "the Nuqtavi coronation and subsequent suppression of the movement marked the official Safavi disavowal of a worldview that had brought them to power a century earlier" (Babayan, *Mystics*, 5). Shah 'Abbas's policies towards the Nuqtavis, therefore, clearly and firmly set Iran on a course that came to favor Shi'i orthodoxy over unorthodox Sufism.

SHAH 'ABBAS AND POLITICAL LEGITIMACY

Shah 'Abbas's chroniclers tell us much about his political agendas and similarly reveal a great deal about their own biases in their histories. A relatively large number of individuals wrote about the reign of Shah 'Abbas. The author of the most polished and official of these narratives was Iskandar Beg Munshi, whose chronicle has already been cited here. A court secretary and eyewitness to many of the events in Shah 'Abbas's life, Iskandar Beg eventually fell out of favor with his teacher, Qazi Ahmad Qummi, who himself wrote the earliest chronicle of Shah 'Abbas's reign. Other significant sources include an account by one of Shah 'Abbas's court astrologers, Munajjim Yazdi, whose history is more reflective of the day-to-day goings-on at court. Afushtah-i Natanzi apparently disapproved of the young monarch and was particularly interested in representing him as if he were a figure in an epic Persian poem. While these chroniclers narrate all or significant portions of Shah 'Abbas's career, some authors focused on just one particular event. For example, the accountant Siyaqi Nizam composed a history solely devoted to Shah 'Abbas's 1598 military campaign against the Uzbeks in Khurasan. When read in a critical fashion, the chronicles tell us a great deal about Shah 'Abbas's attempts to legitimize his rule.

On the basis of these sources, we know that during the first phase of his rule, Shah 'Abbas was still able to draw on traditional notions of Safavid political legitimacy described in chapter 1; the king was being the shadow of God on earth, the representative of the Hidden Imam, and the head of the Safavid Sufi order. For example, in describing Shah 'Abbas's coronation, the chronicler Natanzi draws attention to the fact that the date of the coronation corresponded – according to a system of calculation known as *abjad* that assigns each letter of the alphabet a particular numerical value – to the phrase "shadow of God" (*zill Allah* = 996/1588). He further explains that "just as the shadow of divine compassion encompasses everything other than God, by this analogy, all of the inhabitants of the world and the generality of humankind are under the umbrella of his kingly justice and favor and gain complete protection and tranquility" (Natanzi, *Naqavat*, 283; Arjomand, *Shadow*, 95). Similarly, Iskandar Beg states the following:

> It is in consideration of the dictum "the just ruler is the Shadow of God" (*al-sultan al-'adil zill Allah*), that monarchs are regarded as the shadow of divinity (*rububiyat*) and as a part of prophethood (*nubuvvat*) and viceregency (*vilayat*). God be praised, therefore, that He has chosen as ruler of Iran, which is the choicest part of the inhabited world and the most excellent region of the earth, a king [Shah 'Abbas] who possesses these qualities to perfection.

Iskandar Beg then repeats the same chronogram for Shah 'Abbas's accession as Natanzi, "The Shadow of God," corresponding to 996/1588 (*TAA*, 377–378/547).

Genealogies tracing the family's descent back to the Seventh Imam Musa al-Kazim continued to appear at the beginning of every official or semi-official chronicle produced during Shah 'Abbas's reign, thereby indicating that this form of legitimation was still important.

However, the most ineffective assertion at this time was the idea of the Safavid king claiming authority as the Sufi shaykh. As we have seen, the Qizilbash enjoyed great power when Shah 'Abbas took the throne, and he spent much of this early phase of his reign trying to curb their influence. Rather than continue appealing to the Qizilbash on the basis of being their Sufi shaykh and their king, Shah 'Abbas decided to eliminate those Qizilbash individuals who posed too great a threat, such as Ya'qub Khan, and at the same time focus on establishing the *ghulam* army. Other Sufi groups who would have respected the idea of the "king as shaykh," such as the Ni'matallahis, had either been suppressed or co-opted. This left a legitimizing void of sorts that needed to be filled.

The situation was exacerbated because, in addition to the

internal challenges that Shah 'Abbas faced, rival monarchs of powerful dynasties to his east and west were also launching their own programs of legitimacy and royal authority, some of which Shah 'Abbas appears to have addressed at least indirectly. When it came to displays of royal power coming from the neighboring Ottoman and Mughal monarchs, they ruled from far grander palaces and capital cities. The Ottomans had already, nearly a hundred years ago, captured Constantinople, capital of the Byzantine empire, after centuries of Islamic rulers had tried to do so without success. After this remarkable victory which earned them tremendous prestige, Ottoman sultans ruled from the Topkapi palace in the city they now called Istanbul. Suleyman's gifted architect, Mimar Sinan, had dotted the Ottoman landscape with stunning mosques, creating a distinct Ottoman style already in place by the time Shah 'Abbas was in power. To the east, the Mughals had, just one year before Shah 'Abbas came to power, begun building Fatehpour Sikri, a planned city designed to serve as capital for the Mughal empire. How could the small and comparably insignificant city of Qazvin compete with either of these capitals? Perhaps partly for this reason, Shah 'Abbas moved the capital city to Isfahan, where he began a magnificent building project, so as not to be outdone by his neighbors.

Shah 'Abbas's fellow rulers sought to make the most of their religious accomplishments, which in some cases brought them greater prestige than the Safavids. For the Ottomans, a major source of authority and clout was the fact that they came to control the twin holy cities of Mecca and Medina, as the Ottoman Sultan Selim I had taken these cities in 1516, when Shah Isma'il was in power and long before Shah 'Abbas came to the throne. Through this achievement, the Ottomans had thus enjoyed over half a century of tremendous stature, both political and religious, and they made the most that they could of it, including appending distinguished titles to their names such as "Servant of the Two Holy Sanctuaries," and upholding themselves as the great protectors of Islam.

While the Ottomans were increasingly being viewed as the guardians of Sunni orthodoxy, the Mughal emperor Akbar was engaging in bold religious experiments. These included the construction of a "house of worship" where he hosted debates between representatives of different religious traditions, and an "infallibility decree," in which he gave himself the power to settle religious disputes in cases where theologians disagreed. He also announced the *sulh-i kull* (general or universal peace) in 1579, which attempted to put an end to religious conflict within his kingdom. Finally, in 1581, he proclaimed the *din-i ilahi* ("the divine religion"). This was an imperial cult in which Akbar played the role of something akin to a Sufi leader. A few of his devotees joined the *din-i ilahi* and offered their lives and property and faith in a show of absolute loyalty to the king. Shah 'Abbas apparently did not feel that he was in a strong enough position to risk attacking and offending the Mughals on account of Akbar's innovative religious perspectives. A draft of a letter that he sent to Akbar in 1598 contained a clause in which he "forcefully asserts the truth of the revealed Faith against the religious eclecticism and the doctrine of 'Peace with all' commended by Akbar," but the final version of the letter does not include these details and "assumes Akbar's seniority and his established position as a great ruler" (Islam, *Indo-Persian*, 63).

SHAH 'ABBAS AS "THE SUPREME LORD OF THE AUSPICIOUS CONJUNCTION"

At this stage in his career, Shah 'Abbas could not yet claim prestige by ruling from an impressive capital like his Ottoman counterparts. One of the ways, therefore, that he compensated for this, and for the problems over legitimacy discussed above, was by associating his name and his career with an older famous self-styled world conqueror.

Timur, or Tamerlane, as he is often known in the west, was a Turk from Central Asia who had modeled his career on that of Genghis Khan. Engaging in a long series of military campaigns, he killed thousands of people, erected Mongol-style towers of skulls, and, like Genghis Khan, was deeply admired by later generations who wished to emulate him, or who tried to benefit from his prestige. For example, the Mughals made much of the fact that they were physical descendants of Timur. As for Shah ʻAbbas, one of his chroniclers, Siyaqi Nizam, who narrated Shah ʻAbbas's conquest of Khurasan against the Uzbeks, completed his history just as Shah ʻAbbas was transferring the capital to Isfahan. He seems to have delighted in writing an elaborate introduction to his chronicle in which he put his calculation and accounting skills to unusual and good political use: he linked Shah ʻAbbas to Twelver Shiʻism and Timur by numerical means. He emphasizes Shah ʻAbbas's connection to Twelver Shiʻism, but adds that he would be referring to ʻAbbas as the "Supreme Lord of the Auspicious Conjunction" (*sahib-qiran-i aʻla*) throughout the rest of his account. The title *sahib-qiran-i aʻla* is closely associated with Timur, who used it because he was thought to have been born during a conjunction of the planets Jupiter and Mars. This is what Siyaqi Nizam says:

> The Supreme Lord of the Fortunate Conjunction [Shah ʻAbbas] is the propagator of the true religion of the Twelve Imams, and because of his kinship with the revered True Guides (Imams), and without his design or desire, the major events of his increasingly glorious reign – from his accession to the throne of the sultanate to the royal departure towards various parts of the kingdom – add up to twelve. [And in this, he is] similar to the victorious Lord of the Fortunate Conjunction Amir Timur Kuragan, who would pay no heed to the auspiciousness or inauspiciousness of the time, and would proceed with all matters and manners of kingship, whether good or bad, and then, upon re-examination it would appear that they [his undertakings] had occurred at auspicious times.
>
> (Siyaqi Nizam, *Fotuhat*, 334)

Siyaqi Nizam then notes that the name "Shah ʻAbbas Husayni" and the phrase "Supreme Lord of the Auspicious Conjunction" (*sahib-qiran-i aʻla*) – according to the *abjad* calculation – equal 577, and for this reason he would continue referring to Shah ʻAbbas as *sahib-qiran-i aʻla*, thereby constantly linking Shah ʻAbbas with Timur throughout his chronicle.

The chronicler Qazi Ahmad traces the history of the Safavids back to their Sufi ancestors. In his account of Safavid origins, Qazi Ahmad adds a new element to the standard story of the rise of the Safavids by suggesting that Timur met the second Safaviyya Sufi leader, Shaykh Sadr al-Din. Timur, he says, met Shaykh Sadr al-Din on his way back to Iran from Anatolia, having taken a number of prisoners. Qazi Ahmad says that Shaykh Sadr al-Din was responsible for having those prisoners freed:

> It is said that at the time that Amir Timur Gurkan returned from Anatolia and that region, he was honored by making a pilgrimage to the sepulchre and the holy resting place of Sultan Shaykh Safi al-Din, and reached the *majlis* (gathering) of Sultan Shaykh Sadr al-Din. After being honored at the gathering, he asked that revered one [Shaykh Sadr al-Din], "Do you wish anything from me?" That revered one said, "Give me the group of captives that you brought with you from Anatolia and have imprisoned." Amir Timur, according to the command of that revered one, bestowed that group to him, and from that date, those clans in Anatolia are disciples of the great [Safavid] family and household.
>
> (Qazi Ahmad, *Khulasat*, 32–33)

In other words, Sadr al-Din freed the captives, whose descendants revered the Safavids for ever after. Qazi Ahmad most likely added this story in order to explain the role of Turkomans in the formation of the Safavid dynasty.

These examples point to a specific moment in Safavid history in which Shah 'Abbas experimented with associating himself with Timur. They reflect the kinds of transformations that Safavid kingship was undergoing during the early years of Shah 'Abbas's reign. Later, as he established himself in his new capital city of Isfahan, he also tried to appeal to the new *ghulam* elite, whom he empowered in order to counteract the Qizilbash. As Shah 'Abbas continued to move the monarchy away from the Safavid *ghuluww* past, Iran became increasingly orthodox in its Shi'i religious character and identity. The king's construction of a new capital in Isfahan only helped facilitate that transformation.

3

BUILDING HALF THE WORLD: 1598–1612

The Isfahan phase of Shah 'Abbas's rule, from 1598 to 1612, forms the most significant period of his reign. By this time, he was in a position to transform his empire in ways that allowed it to compete with neighboring Ottomans and Mughals for prestige, wealth, and territory, and to centralize his rule. In building a spectacular new capital in Isfahan, few aspects of life in Iran were unaffected by Shah 'Abbas's policies. Here, we will focus on Shah 'Abbas's building of Isfahan and some of the equally important social and economic transformations that accompanied the establishment of the new capital. Subsequent chapters will focus on religion, foreign relations, and artistic developments during the Isfahan phase.

Of all the jewels in the Safavid crown, none dazzled more brilliantly than the city of Isfahan. Isfahan – a product of Shah 'Abbas's imagination and creativity – still stands as one of the most beautiful cities in Iran and indeed all of the Middle East. Ever since Isfahan's establishment as the Safavid capital, travelers and tourists visited and praised the city, as did local residents. Della Valle favorably compared the city to Istanbul, the capital of the Ottoman empire:

> This city is very large, handsome, and well peopled, so much so that in all of the east I have met with none which excel it; for notwithstanding in point of situation Constantinople certainly surpasses, in many other points it falls short of Hisfahan [Isfahan].
>
> (Della Valle, 29–30/23)

Although Isfahan was not yet complete when Della Valle went there, he imagined the even greater impact it would have upon visitors upon its completion, this time giving it the advantage over Istanbul: "When complete I conceive that the circuit of the whole will be superior to that of Constantinople or Rome" (Della Valle, 29–30/23). One of Shah 'Abbas's own chroniclers compared Isfahan to Tabriz, seat of the first capital of the Safavid dynasty: "Isfahan became such a 'capital city' that, next to it, Tabriz, despite its wealth of beauty and its abundance of attractive and decent people, appeared a decidedly provincial town" (McChesney, "Sources," 106, slightly modified translation).

Isfahan was, however, much more than simply a beautiful city that Iranians today still refer to as *nisf-i jahan*, or "half the world." The king's mosque (*masjid-i shah*), the 'Ali Qapu gateway, the Shaykh Lutf Allah Mosque, the grand bazaar, and the other building projects that Shah 'Abbas sponsored not only reveal the aesthetics of architecture and artistic creativity fostered in the Safavid period, but they also reflect notions of Safavid kingship and authority, the relationship between religion and the state, and the position of commerce and trade in Iran. It is to these themes, therefore, and Shah 'Abbas's role in them, that we now turn, by taking a tour of the main edifices and structures that Shah 'Abbas built in Isfahan.

Isfahan's location, towards the center of Iran and, more importantly, farther away from the Ottomans and Uzbeks, along with the abundant water flowing in the Zayandah river, made it more suitable than Qazvin for a capital city. The city was not built from scratch, nor was it a static, unchanging place. Isfahan, the origins of which go back to Achaemenid times, already contained gardens and structures dating to the eleventh-century Seljuq period. But as a capital city for the Safavids, it was built in stages and the purposes intended for the city changed over time. Shah 'Abbas began the project literally in the center, starting with the great royal square known as the "Image of the World Square" (*maydan-i naqsh-i jahan*). It is also sometimes referred to as the King's Square (*maydan-i shah*) or simply the Square (*maydan*). With the square forming the city's centerpiece, the shah commissioned the most important buildings around its perimeter. These included the Royal Mosque, the Shaykh Lutf Allah Mosque (the Dome Mosque), the 'Ali Qapu gateway, and the bazaar, or Qaysariya.

THE IMAGE OF THE WORLD SQUARE

The Image of the World Square of Isfahan is one of the largest public squares in the world. It appears to have been built in two phases that reflect its two different functions: during the first phase, the Safavids used the square for sports and entertainment, and during the second phase, it became a place primarily for trade and commerce and the reception of foreign envoys and their suites. The first phase of construction lasted from 1590 until 1595. During this time, workers leveled the square, poured down sand, planted gardens in each corner, and decorated the walls. The square measured approximately 440 × 160 yards.

Once construction was completed, Shah 'Abbas held polo games, firework displays, and other sorts of festivities there. At times, the square was closed to men so that women could engage in commercial activity. It also became a site for public executions. The Safavid chronicler Natanzi describes in detail the sorts of flamboyant public displays that took place in the *maydan*. In one instance, he lists some twenty-two different types of firework effects that were used in what must have been a spectacular pyrotechnic exhibit. The fireworks had evocative names such as starburst, pineapples, peacock's fan, magic narcissus, Indian rose, seven-colored narcissus, and salamander flower. More significantly, Natanzi also describes a performance that took place as part of one evening's entertainment after such a firework display, where spectators were treated to a historical reenactment of the victorious Safavid campaign against the Uzbeks (to be discussed in chapter 5). For the reenactment, an elaborate construction of four "battlements" complete with "towers and parapets" on each side of the square was erected, each containing some one hundred effigies of Qizilbash and Uzbeks decked out in "purple and red dress with all the equipment of war" (McChesney, "Sources," 108). The performance opened with Uzbeks and Qizilbash attempting unsuccessfully to engage in pre-war negotiations. This was followed by a reenactment of the battle itself, after which they set the battlements on fire, which created so much smoke that the stars were barely visible. In sponsoring such an extravagant pageant on the square, Shah 'Abbas reinforced his victory over the Uzbeks, and demonstrated that the Safavids were important world players in the political space they inhabited.

The second phase of development, which began sometime around 1603, emphasized the commercial aspect of the square. During this period, the square became something approximating an open air shopping mall, as it was reconfigured with additional upper galleries and a second floor on the walls of the square to accommodate more shops and coffee houses. During both phases, Shah 'Abbas spent a great deal of time in the square and enjoyed the activities taking place there.

In addition to the formal celebrations such as the firework show that accompanied the pageant commemorating the victory against the Uzbeks, informal events and activities also took place on the square. Della Valle observed Shah 'Abbas in that space after its second phase of construction, noting that he:

> every day rides out also on horseback into the middle of the Meidan, when sometimes he amuses himself in conversing with each individual; at others exercises his horse backwards and forwards on the square; at others again, listens to any one who wishes to address him. Occasionally he has refreshments brought him into the middle of the square. Now he takes an airing in a different part, accompanied by his courtiers; at other times, and most frequently, he rides by himself among the bazaars, to see what is passing.
>
> (Della Valle, 38/26)

In another instance, the Carmelite missionaries Father Benignus and Father Redempt, who visited Iran in 1609, happened to be at the square during a spontaneous animal fight:

> In order to amuse the Shah, some poor people had brought on to the Maidan a number of rams, which had been trained to fight one another, charging with great fury: each of the men (who had brought them) had an immense ambition that his own ram should come off the victor: and so the animals had long and furious contests, in which the Shah took much pleasure.
>
> (*Carmelites* I, 184)

THE KING'S PALACE

On the western side of the royal square Shah ʻAbbas built an impressive structure known as the "Sublime Gateway" (*EIR*, "Ali Qapu"). Like other buildings on the square, the gate edifice was constructed in phases and stages, not reaching its final form until after his death. As Della Valle notes, the ʻAli Qapu, as the entry to the king's palace, was viewed as sacred:

> When the King comes hither it is always on horseback, through a wide alley between two rows of very high walls, reaching from the gate of entrance to the palace where he resides. The utmost reverence is shewn to the gate of entrance, so much so, that no one presumes to tread on a certain step of wood in it somewhat elevated, but, on the contrary, people kiss it occasionally as a precious and holy thing.
>
> (Della Valle, 35–36/25–26)

Attached to the gate was a large multi-level square structure. The ʻAli Qapu served a number of purposes, but most frequently it hosted the king's formal receptions and other state functions. These took place in the upper levels, while the lower level housed administrative offices and served as a gateway through which one could reach the palace complex edifices situated off the main square. Among the individuals situated here were the chief judge, the grand master of the household, the chief of the gate keepers, and the grand vizier. Shah 'Abbas himself held audience at the 'Ali Qapu. Father Simon, another Carmelite, notes how quickly Shah 'Abbas dispensed justice there:

> He is very speedy in dispatching business: when he gives audience, which he does at the gate of his palace, in the Maidan, he finishes off all the cases that are brought to him. The parties stand present before him, the officers of justice and his own council, with whom he consults when it pleases him. The sentence which he gives is final and is immediately executed.
>
> (*Carmelites* I, 159)

Although the great balcony that one sees today as part of the 'Ali Qapu was probably built later during the reign of Shah 'Abbas II, the roof of the building at the time of Shah 'Abbas still afforded wonderful views of the polo games and other festivities taking place on the great square.

The colorful murals that decorate the interior of the 'Ali Qapu reflect the prevailing court culture under Shah 'Abbas. Della Valle, in a somewhat disapproving tone, describes its paintings:

> All their pictures are representations of men and women, either single or together, in lascivious postures standing, drinking with bottles and cups in their hands; some overcome with wine and sleeping, others reeling, in short, displays of the votaries of Venus and Bacchus. Among these, mostly drest in the costume of the country, are some with hats, intended to represent Europeans, apparently designed to intimate that Persians are not the only ones addicted to wine. These figures, notwithstanding they be painted in extremely rich colours, are badly drawn, the painters of the country being far from ours ...
>
> (Della Valle, 36–37/26)

The king's palace complex itself was situated in an area known as the *dawlatkhana* (royal precincts), which housed various palaces, pavilions, administrative quarters, and the royal harem. The *dawlatkhana* stretched alongside the Chahar Bagh (literally "four gardens"), a public garden-avenue that crossed the Zayandah river and went over the Allahverdi Khan bridge. The bridge connected the city's new section to the older neighborhoods, and was one of a number of structures, including roads and caravanserais, built by *ghulam* governors.

Although Isfahan contained numerous mosques, two in particular are associated with Shah 'Abbas and the royal square: the Royal Mosque and the Shaykh Lutf Allah Mosque.

THE ROYAL MOSQUE

Directly opposite the Qaysariya stood the Royal Mosque (*Masjid-i shah*), also known as the New Abbasi Mosque (*Masjid-i jadid-i Abbasi*). Work on this massive congregational mosque where the Friday congregational prayer was held, the first ever built by a Safavid monarch, commenced in 1611. The building of this mosque signified the resolution of a longstanding debate regarding the permissibility of saying the Friday prayer in the absence of the Hidden Imam, a debate that will be discussed in greater detail in chapter 5. The Royal Mosque was situated on the southern side of the square and the most impressive structure in that area.

Shah 'Abbas's efforts to acquire the land for the mosque became the stuff of legend, as various sources relate different stories about how this came to pass. The chronicler Munajjim Yazdi, the king's royal court astrologer, emphasizes Shah 'Abbas's fairness, generosity, and respect for individuals' property when he describes how the king purchased the private homes standing on the land where he wanted to build the mosque. Despite the king's desire for this land, one homeowner, an elderly mulla, refused to sell his property. When Shah 'Abbas found out about the situation from the architect Badi al-Zaman, he stated, "Calm [the old man], but don't lay a finger on the house without his consent" (McChesney, "Sources," 110). Badi al-Zaman decided to construct a new house away from the area where the mosque was to be built. This new house contained, among other amenities, a kitchen and running water, and was landscaped with fruit trees and flowers. When the old man saw the home, he wished it could be his. The architect consequently presented it to the old man as a gift. Shah 'Abbas paid the man the value of his old dwelling and presented him and his son with royal garments. He also paid the architect the price of the house. This story must have captured the imagination of those who heard it, as it was retold over time, albeit with different details. Robert McChesney suggests that the persistence of the story reflects the sanctity of private land holding in the face of royal plans for development of the square (McChesney, "Sources," 121–122).

In terms of the actual construction, decoration, and ornamentation of the mosque, a number of artisans and craftsmen lent their expertise to the project, with stunning effect. The chief architect/engineer was 'Ali Akbar al-Isfahani. The mosque contains a large number of inscriptions, both religious and financial in nature. Some passages, for example, praise God and Muhammad, but others consist of statements regarding how Shah 'Abbas abolished or lowered taxes for various groups of individuals. The technique used in the construction of the mosque itself consisted of a newer and faster way of firing the multicolored bricks that adorned its exterior. The result was a striking tile mosaic of turquoise, yellow, white, and cobalt blue, forming abstract floral designs and Arabic inscriptions that completely covered the dome and entrance of the mosque. The same process, which made it possible to use a more extensive color palette, was used on the 'Ali Qapu, the bazaar gate, and the second mosque situated on the royal square, the Shaykh Lutf Allah Mosque.

The Royal Mosque was huge, housing two Islamic schools (madrasas) within its complex. Its strategic location meant that the people of the city had to pass the Qaysariya area of the square both on their way to the mosque and on their way back from it. In a manner reminiscent of modern marketing practices, Shah 'Abbas thereby redirected traffic so that people would pass by enticing shops on their way to and from prayers at the mosque. In this way, he quite literally connected the commercial and religious functions of the square. The mosque also served as political propaganda for Shah 'Abbas. In building the Royal Mosque, he was also indirectly stating that he – and not the clerical classes that were becoming increasingly powerful during his reign – was the primary sponsor of public worship in Isfahan.

THE SHAYKH LUTF ALLAH MOSQUE

Directly opposite the 'Ali Qapu gateway stood the Shaykh Lutf Allah Mosque, the first edifice to be constructed on the square. Completed in 1618, this mosque was named after Shaykh Lutf Allah, Shah 'Abbas's father-in-law and a Shi'i scholar from the Jabal 'Amil region of Syria, in present-day southern Lebanon. Shaykh Lutf Allah came to Iran during the reign of Shah Tahmasb. He ended up in Qazvin after escaping the Uzbek invasions of Mashhad in 1589, and went to Isfahan at Shah 'Abbas's request. Eventually, Shah 'Abbas married his daughter and she became part of the royal harem.

While the Royal Mosque served as a place of public worship, the purpose of the smaller Shaykh Lutf Allah Mosque is unclear; some of the sources suggest that it was intended as a place for the shaykh himself to teach and pray, but other sources state that the mosque took on the shaykh's name only after he established himself there. Either way, Shah 'Abbas used the mosque for his own private worship, as reflected in an inscription on the exterior of the mosque, introducing the edifice as "the blessed mosque of the great sultan". Another inscription refers to Shah 'Abbas as the "propagator of the faith of the Infallible Imams," thereby emphasizing the king's central and authoritative role in the consolidation of Twelver Shi'ism in Iran (*EIR*, "Isfahan x. Monuments (3) Mosques"). Despite its much greater size, the Royal Mosque does not overshadow the Shaykh Lutf Allah Mosque, largely because of the striking tile work covering the entire exterior, especially the dome. The mosque's dome is covered in tiles of turquoise, beige, and white, and arranged in intricate floral and arabesque motifs. In situating a public mosque and a private mosque on opposite sides of the royal square, Shah 'Abbas brilliantly appropriated into royal space both public religiosity for the population of Isfahan and space for his own private religious devotions, and connected both to his royal palace and the economic center of the square: the royal bazaar.

THE ROYAL BAZAAR

On one end of the square stood the great bazaar, and nowhere in Isfahan were Shah 'Abbas's economic policies better reflected. This bazaar, known as the Qaysariya, or the *bazzaz khan* ("cloth house"), dates back to 1590 or 1592 and the establishment of the square itself. Although markets existed in Isfahan before Shah 'Abbas started transforming the city, his decision to establish a new bazaar on the square indicates the thought and care that he put into economic matters. Initially, he had planned to renovate the old existing markets in the city, but highly placed and powerful local elites opposed the idea. As a result, he rather quickly changed his plans and built a new commercial center directly on the maydan. Natanzi explains that Shah 'Abbas himself commanded the construction of the bazaar:

> He gave an order to create a qaysariya structure like the one that was [once?] located in Tabriz. He rebuilt all the old bazaars and designed many shops and chahār suqs. In a short time all were completed. The craft guilds, following each other's examples, adorned the shops with a vast variety of goods.
>
> (McChesney, "Sources," 106)

One entered the bazaar through a massive entrance known as the Qaysariya gateway, perhaps the most striking aspect of the bazaar. This semi-circular gateway had five sides and contained a pool. Lively murals of Shah 'Abbas engaged in various traditional kingly activities such as hunting and enjoying victory against the Uzbeks, together with a painting of Sagittarius, in whose month Isfahan was established, decorated the upper sections of the gateway. The balconies of the gateway were reserved for musicians who played the drums and trumpet at sunset and midnight. Through the gateway was the bazaar proper, where merchants displayed and sold all manner of goods, including metal ware, jewelry, and a variety of textiles such as silks, linens, and golden threaded cloths. Along with display shops, the bazaar also contained an imperial mint and the king's caravanserai, both structures essential to the economic life of Isfahan. Economically, the bazaar was a success both for Shah 'Abbas – as the rents from the shops went to him – and for the Safavid empire, as it helped trade to flourish.

ENDOWMENTS

Shah 'Abbas took several steps in order to increase his commercial power and keep the royal square area financially sound. His involvement in this activity indicates his desire and willingness to shape Isfahan's commercial status in order to create a suitable imperial capital. One of his most important policies was to make the entire royal square complex part of a religious/pious foundation (*waqf*), an endowment that he dedicated to the Twelve Shi'i Imams. The funds that came in from the foundation were then re-invested in the commercial enterprises of the square. As a result of the funding it received and the stability which that financial support accorded, the new bazaar gained an advantage over the old commercial area and became an attractive alternative for merchants wanting to sell their goods. Shah 'Abbas further stipulated that future kings should appoint the administrator of the endowment, thereby ensuring continuity and security for current and future tenants in the bazaar.

In addition to endowing the square and constructing the necessary edifices to house merchants and promote commerce, Shah 'Abbas also instituted numerous policies designed to encourage trade and commerce in his capital city, and to improve the general economy. Together these significantly transformed Safavid society and the Safavid economy.

SOCIAL TRANSFORMATIONS: THE ARMENIANS AND NEW JULFA

In addition to building a new square with edifices designed to impress, Shah 'Abbas also built an entirely new neighborhood in order to house the Armenians that he had forcibly transferred to Isfahan. His reasons for doing this were economic, but the episode also had significant social ramifications. Silk was the most important commercial product for Shah 'Abbas, and the community of Armenians that he resettled in Isfahan, who had long been involved in the silk export trade in their region of origin in Armenia, became intimately connected with silk trade and production – now under the supervision of the Safavid state. Shah 'Abbas's interventions in the silk trade, along with the silk policy that he eventually established, were part of his attempts to increase state revenue, centralize his rule, and strengthen his hand against the Ottomans. It was within this context that he forcibly moved a group of Armenians from the Armenian town of Julfa to Isfahan, where they ultimately settled in a neighborhood called "New Julfa."

The resettlement of the Armenians of Julfa was part of a longstanding tradition of relocating whole populations from one end of the country to the other that dates back at least to Iran's pre-Islamic Achaemenid period, when kings such as Cambyses and Darius resettled Egyptian and Barcean populations. The reasons for engaging in this practice varied, but often it was done in order to suppress rebellious populations or to take advantage of the craftsmanship skills of a particular group of people. The Armenians were not the only population that Shah 'Abbas relocated; communities from India and northern Iran were also transferred to the new capital, and Jews to Gilan and Mazandaran. They were, however, the most important group that Shah 'Abbas moved for the sake of bolstering Isfahan's economic life, and they came to play an important role in the silk business.

The campaign that brought the Armenians to Isfahan took place in the aftermath of the context of the peace treaty, described above in chapter 2, that Shah 'Abbas was forced to sign in 1590, which gave the Ottomans control of Azerbaijan, Transcaucasia, and Armenia. By 1603, Shah 'Abbas was ready to retake that territory. Ottoman rule over these regions had resulted in considerable discontent and even rebellion; local populations therefore hoped that the Safavids would improve their situation.

In the midst of his campaign against the Ottomans, as will be described in greater detail in chapter 5, Shah 'Abbas had successfully captured Tabriz, Nakhjavan, and Yerevan. As this was happening, the Ottomans started deploying troops towards Yerevan. Rather than directly confront the Ottomans, Shah 'Abbas commanded his army to retreat. It was at this juncture that he ordered the destruction of towns and cities and the depopulation and the transfer of large numbers of people in the region back to Iran, especially from Julfa. His decision to do this had a significant impact on the future of the Safavid economy, and of course on the lives of those who were displaced. Historians have disagreed to some extent as to whether or not Shah 'Abbas intended to transfer the Julfans to Isfahan as part of a pre-planned economic policy or as a more spontaneous decision. Sebouh Aslanian suggests that the deportations "appear to be the outcome of *improvised* decisions taken in response to a series of contingent events" (Aslanian, *Indian Ocean*, 34). In making the decisions that led to the transfer of this community to his new capital, Shah 'Abbas displayed one of his most impressive political talents: his ability to think quickly on his feet and manipulate circumstances to his advantage as events developed and changed over time.

An Armenian chronicler by the name of Arak'el, writing in the late seventeenth century, describes the events and Shah 'Abbas's role in them in considerable detail from an Armenian perspective. Arak'el's history, covering the years 1602–1662, describes how Shah 'Abbas initially spent three days in Julfa, enjoying the hospitality and the kingly reception that the Julfans gave him. But Shah 'Abbas then lay siege to Yerevan, and charged Hanis Tahmasb-Quli Beg, an Armenian *ghulam* convert to Islam, with the job of expelling the population of Julfa from the city. The town crier in Julfa announced the following expulsion orders from Shah 'Abbas:

> The great king, Shah 'Abbas, orders you to leave and move to the land of the Persians. If you move within three days, we shall treat you leniently. Those who are found here after three days will be killed and their families and their belongings will become captives. If anyone flees or hides, his property shall be given to the person who points him out and his head will be sent to the shah.
>
> (Arak'el, *History*, 50)

After throwing the keys to their church into the river, the townspeople left Julfa, crossed the Arax river, and made their way to Tabriz, Qazvin, and eventually Isfahan. Shah 'Abbas then ordered Julfa to be set on fire and the town's buildings to be destroyed:

> They immediately went to Julfa with large bands, carrying burning torches, reeds, and lamps full of *nafta*, and began to set fire to everything. They pulled down roofs and houses built of stone. Not a single structure remained standing; everything was destroyed and ruined.
>
> (Arak'el, *History*, 52)

Upon being forced out of Julfa between 21 October and 19 November 1604, the Julfans were taken to Tabriz, then Qazvin for the winter, and finally were sent to Isfahan in the spring of 1605.

In the end, several thousand Julfans were eventually moved to an area south of the Zayandah river in Isfahan. There, in New Julfa, they settled and formed a self-contained community. They initially spent some time in Isfahan proper, but several months later Shah 'Abbas gave the order for them to be moved to their permanent home due to tensions and conflict between the Julfans and the local Muslim populations. Once settled in their suburb, the Armenians built several churches, including the famous Vank Cathedral. They also established New Julfa as a trading "nodal center" and, over time, ran four “circuits” of trade, with settlements in the Indian Ocean, Russia, the Mediterranean, and northwestern Europe (Aslanian, *Indian Ocean*, 44, 216). The Julfans, together with the *ghulams*, expanded and increased the Safavid silk trade, particularly through exporting silk to Europe via the Ottoman empire. This boosted the economic power of the shah, who received a certain percentage of the profits.

Shah ‘Abbas, who knew the Armenians’ reputation as excellent traders in old Julfa, also used them for diplomatic and commercial purposes outside Iran. He established a relationship whereby they answered to him via a mayor, or *kalantar*. The *kalantar* had several functions, including acting as liaison between the king and the Julfans and serving as head of the Armenian community. In this way, Shah ‘Abbas could keep the community under his supervision, yet at the same time grant the Armenians local autonomy.

Along with exporting silk, the Armenians also imported silver, which was used to pay for goods such as silk and to finance military campaigns, into the Safavid empire, as there were no mines of gold or silver in Iran. In 1618, Shah ‘Abbas banned the export from Iran of gold and silver that had entered the country, a measure which, together with the silk monopoly (which we will discuss in chapter 7), he instituted in order to consolidate his state and establish political control over his domains. While the ban was not successful – as silver made its way out of the empire, especially into India – it paid for cotton and precious stones coming from Mughal territory. As a result, the relationship between the Julfan Armenians and Mughal India became quite strong, and the revenues that came into Iran helped finance Shah ‘Abbas’s military and administrative reforms.

SOCIAL TRANSFORMATIONS: THE SAFAVID HOUSEHOLD IN ISFAHAN

While the Armenians of New Julfa emerged as a new elite in Isfahan that enjoyed direct ties to the court, they were not alone in benefiting from their new status. Isfahan hosted a newly fashioned royal household in which *ghulams*, eunuchs, and concubines held power, and *ghulams* were part of the new elite. Eventually, some four thousand *ghulams* and eunuchs were at the court. The Armenians also formed part of the new elite. Shah 'Abbas enjoyed better relations with these new elements in Safavid society than with the old Qizilbash elite. *Ghulams* replaced the Qizilbash as provincial governors, but such individuals also kept houses in Isfahan, which served to strengthen their ties with the king.

Another significant transformation that took place in the Safavid household was that princes became confined to the harem – the area of the palace where the women and children lived. Previously, royal princes were dispatched to the provinces where, under the supervision of governors, they gained valuable "on-the-job" experience in governing. Now, these princes lived in the palace, supervised by their mothers, and guarded by eunuchs. In the new system, then, all of these groups derived power due to their physical proximity to the king and hence the center of authority. While royal princes lost valuable training, their presence at court put them in a position to form coalitions with others residing at the palace. This in turn led Shah 'Abbas to harbor suspicions about their designs on the throne, which ultimately resulted in his having all of his sons blinded or murdered, as will be discussed in chapter 7.

GENERAL ECONOMIC POLICIES AND MEASURES

Less visible than the impressive buildings on the square or the new neighborhood of New Julfa, but just as important, were the measures Shah 'Abbas took to generate revenue for the state and to improve the infrastructure necessary for trade.

He did this in a number of ways. While the most visible, perhaps, was his establishment of the Armenians in the silk trade, he also engaged in land reform. As a result of suppressing the Qizilbash,

Shah 'Abbas was able to take provincial land administered by governors such as Ya'qub Khan and turn such property into crown land. In this way, revenue that previously had gone to the provincial governor went directly to the crown, and was used to do things such as paying court officials and administrators, and financing the building of Isfahan and the king's military campaigns. In addition to promoting trade in order to stimulate the economy, he also established policies that encouraged local production of goods and food. For example, he promoted growing cotton in Iran and wearing cloth produced from local cotton. This would reduce the amount of Indian cloth coming into the country. Probably for similar reasons, he encouraged the cultivation of Bengal rice.

In order to allow goods to move more freely through his empire, he built a network of caravanserais along the primary trade roads. He also took measures to ensure that the roads already existing were safe. Iskandar Beg places great emphasis on this latter measure, listing it as one of Shah 'Abbas's eleven kingly virtues. According to the chronicler, Shah 'Abbas had some highway robbers arrested, while he forgave and pardoned others. In this way, the roads became secure and "merchants and tradesmen traveled to and from the Safavid empire" (*TAA*, 1104/523).

SHAH 'ABBAS IN ISFAHAN

Although the striking architecture situated around the great square of Isfahan created an appropriately imposing imperial image for Shah 'Abbas, in many ways it was the king himself who made the greatest contribution to that image. He appears to have genuinely enjoyed spending time in his capital city and among its inhabitants, as a number of travelers and visitors to Isfahan have attested. His style of kingship in Isfahan, in contrast to the formal and majestic buildings that he had erected in the royal square, was informal and personal. The Carmelite Father Simon describes the nature of Shah 'Abbas's interactions with the population of Isfahan:

> He will go through the public streets, eat from what they are selling there and other things, speak at ease freely with the lower classes, cause his subjects to remain sitting while he himself is standing, or will sit down beside this man and that. He says that is how to be a king, and that the king of Spain and other Christians do not get any pleasure out of ruling, because they are obliged to comport themselves with so much pomp and majesty as they do.
>
> (*Carmelites* I, 158)

Shah 'Abbas was able to build Isfahan, a stunning capital city, and use it both to house a new, loyal elite class and to establish conditions conducive to trade and commerce. In this phase of his kingship, he was even able to use religion to his political advantage, as we will discuss in the next chapter.

4

RELIGION AND POWER IN ISFAHAN

Shah 'Abbas's great square of Isfahan and the buildings on it were an extension of how he wanted to represent himself: as a powerful, pious king in control of his own public image, the economy, and the religious establishment. It is to this last theme of religion that we now turn. During the Isfahan phase of his reign, Shah 'Abbas tried to the greatest extent possible to show that he was a devout Shi'i as much as a ruler who was above religious laws. This makes it difficult, if not impossible, to have a true understanding of his own personal religiosity, as so much of what he did was part of a "performance of monarchy" intended for public consumption. Thus, he frequently used religion to further his own political agenda, as seen in his pilgrimage on foot to Mashhad. He also maintained a relationship with the Shi'i clergy who had been engaged in converting Iran long before he came to power. This was more complicated than maintaining his public image. Ultimately, he managed to preserve an equilibrium that benefited both himself and the religious scholars (*'ulama*), and allowed a new and important philosophical movement to flourish. Shah 'Abbas's interactions with religious figures went beyond the Shi'i clergy. He showed his pragmatic and ecumenical side in his relationship with Christians, for the policies he directed towards Christians were often based more on expediency than on any sort of absolute religious convictions he may have personally held.

THE PILGRIMAGE ON FOOT TO MASHHAD

Whatever inclinations Shah 'Abbas may have had towards the Nuqtavis and other unorthodox modes of religious expression earlier in his reign, he ultimately set Iran on a course that steered it away from its *ghuluww* past. His pilgrimage in 1601 to the city of Mashhad, resting place of Imam Riza, the Eighth Imam of the Twelver Shi'a, symbolizes this transformation, and demonstrates how Shah 'Abbas was able to use public acts of religious piety to further his political and economic ambitions.

The reason why Shah 'Abbas went to Mashhad at all was because it was on the way to Balkh, where he was headed on a military campaign against the Uzbeks, but Shah 'Abbas's chroniclers explain how the king journeyed from Isfahan to Mashhad in order to fulfill a vow. The exact nature of the vow was unclear, however. This was not his first pilgrimage, as he had made numerous trips to Ardabil to visit the shrine of his ancestors and had been to Mashhad before, on occasion even entering the city on foot. But what made the 1601 pilgrimage unique was the fact that he determined to travel the entire way from Isfahan to Mashhad – a distance of over 700 miles – on foot. Mashhad was on the way to Balkh, the king's ultimate destination for a military campaign against the Uzbeks.

Shah 'Abbas set off from Isfahan on 13 September 1601, while members of his entourage measured the daily distance he covered with a rope. Making stops en route from Isfahan to Mashhad, Shah 'Abbas spent approximately sixty-six days on the journey, which meant he walked about eleven miles a day. He had to deal with a few incidents during his trip, such as the illness of his aunt, Zaynab Begum, which caused him to backtrack to Isfahan from Kashan. Upon making it back to Kashan, with his now-recovered aunt accompanying him, the arrival of a Russian ambassador and a Christian delegation again caused delays. In Kashan, two Nuqtavis joined him on the trip, but along the way, Shah 'Abbas learned about their beliefs, and as if to make a last symbolic break with his past religious interests, he had them and their followers shot in a caravanserai. Shah 'Abbas finally arrived in Mashhad in the winter. Once there, he engaged in pious activities, participating in religious services and "performing various menial tasks at the shrine such as snuffing the candles" (*TAA*, 612/801). He spent the winter in Mashhad before continuing on to Balkh.

Why would Shah 'Abbas make such a journey? Iskandar Beg Munshi provides perhaps the "official" interpretation of the pilgrimage by comparing Shah 'Abbas's journey to one allegedly undertaken by Heraclius, the Byzantine emperor in power during the time of the Prophet Muhammad, from Constantinople to Jerusalem. Although evidence indicates that Heraclius did not in actuality walk this entire distance, Iskandar Beg makes much of the fact that Heraclius's pilgrimage was slow in pace and luxurious in comparison to that of Shah 'Abbas. In making this comparison, Iskandar Beg represents Shah 'Abbas as an imperial ruler who was more devout and pious in his religious devotion than a major Christian ruler of a vast empire that also, and perhaps not coincidentally, happened to encompass territory that later became part of the Ottoman empire.

Despite the official Safavid characterization of the pilgrimage as a purely religious undertaking, Charles Melville has suggested that Shah 'Abbas had a variety of economic, political, and religious motives in walking to Mashhad (Melville, "Pilgrimage," 195–199). He may have been inspired by the Mughal emperor Akbar, whose reign coincided with his own and who used to walk – usually part of the way and on one occasion the entire distance of approximately 230 miles in sixteen days – from Agra to the shrine of the Sufi saint Mu'in al-Din Chishti in Ajmer. Shah 'Abbas's primary economic goal may have been to increase the traffic to Mashhad in order to re-develop the economy of Khurasan in the aftermath of his wars against the Uzbeks. Politically, Shah 'Abbas would have benefited from supporting eastern Iran at a time when pilgrimage to the Shi'i shrines of Iraq and to Mecca and Medina was impossible, due to conflicts with the Ottomans, although he did eventually visit the sites in Iraq after he had taken Baghdad from the Ottomans in 1624. Finally, by emphasizing pilgrimages to places within Safavid territory, Shah 'Abbas could ensure that much-needed revenue would stay within Iran's borders. While it remains unclear whether or not Shah 'Abbas intended that Mashhad serve as an official pilgrimage alternative for the people of Iran, his pilgrimage on foot highlighted Mashhad and allowed him to patronize the shrine. Moreover, in welcoming pilgrims from Central Asia to Mashhad, Shah 'Abbas gained prestige on the international scene.

SHAH 'ABBAS AND THE 'AMILI CLERGY

While making the pilgrimage to Mashhad may have reinforced Shah 'Abbas's image as a pious and devoted Shi'i Muslim, his relationship with the clerics was more complicated. As the process of "converting Iran" continued during Shah 'Abbas's reign and Safavid Shi'ism transformed itself with the help of a rising clerical class, the relationship of king to cleric was, as Rula Jurdi Abisaab has recently put it, "a controlled process of cooperation and resistance" (Abisaab, *Converting*, 55).

In a sense, Shah 'Abbas inherited the successes and problems that resulted from Shah Isma'il's establishment of Shi'ism as the official state religion. By the time he took the throne, orthodox Shi'ism had entered and started to dominate a religious sphere that had previously consisted primarily of folk Shi'ism and Sufism. The report of the Carmelites' visit to Iran during Shah 'Abbas's time describes the increasing power of the clerics:

> They have two kinds of persons dedicated to God's service: one they call "Mullas," which is to say "learned men" or "doctors" ... they are esteemed by the lords and the rest, and have mosques in their charge. The other kind of persons devoted to their charge they call "Darwish" and they profess to abandon the world more (than the other).
>
> (*Carmelites* I, 156–157)

As this passage indicates, it was the clerics or mullas who enjoyed the king's favor in this phase of his rule, rather than Sufis or dervishes. One of the most important groups of Shi'i clerics were those who came to Iran from outside the country, most notably the Jabal 'Amil region in Syria (modern-day southern Lebanon). Shah 'Abbas needed them to help educate the large number of *ghulams* who were converted to Islam upon their arrival in Iran and to continue the process of converting Iran to orthodox Shi'ism. He also may have been trying to give Iran a uniquely Shi'i identity in order to draw distinctions between his Safavid state and the Ottomans. At the same time, however, he also tried to keep the clerics under fairly close supervision and control, and prevent them from behaving too independently.

SYSTEMATIZING ORTHODOX SHI'ISM: SHAYKH BAHA'I

Among the tasks that the 'Amili clerics undertook, upon settling in Iran, was explicating the rituals and tenets of Shi'ism in a simple and clear language, and systematizing and codifying Shi'i jurisprudence. Shah 'Abbas himself spearheaded these efforts in order to make Shi'i doctrine and belief accessible to a large number of people, taking advantage of the talented and gifted scholars who established themselves in Isfahan after he moved the capital there. One of the main individuals associated with this project was Shaykh Baha' al-Din al-'Amili, better known as Shaykh Baha'i.

Shaykh Baha'i, in the words of Iskandar Beg Munshi and in the eyes of many of his contemporaries, was "the foremost scholar of his age" (*TAA*, 157/249). Born in Jabal 'Amil, he came to Iran at a young age with his father, whom Shah Tahmasb appointed as Shaykh al-Islam, or foremost religious administrator, of a number of cities where he promoted Twelver Shi'ism. Shaykh Baha'i himself attained significant religious positions at a fairly young age. He did not become prominent, however, until Shah 'Abbas transferred the capital to Isfahan, at which time he became the Shaykh al-Islam of that city. The extent of Shaykh Baha'i's influence can be seen in the fact that his own poetry forms part of the inscriptions of the Shaykh Lutf Allah Mosque, and that other Shi'i clerics viewed him as not just another from among their ranks, but as a "renewer" (*mujaddid*), a figure who was prophesied, according to a hadith, to appear at the beginning of every century in order to renew the religion. Beyond the great respect he commanded among his clerical peers, Shaykh Baha'i also enjoyed a close relationship with the king. Iskandar Beg tells us that "the Shah kept him constantly at his side; both when he was in the capital and when he was making a journey somewhere, the Shah would visit his dwelling to enjoy his company" (*TAA*, 157/249).

While Shah 'Abbas appreciated Shaykh Baha'i's friendship, the shaykh's own attitudes towards royalty and the court were surprisingly ambivalent or even downright hostile, as when he stated, "If my father had not come to Persia, I would not have been afflicted with the company of the Shah" (Quoted in Abisaab, *Converting*, 59–60). Shaykh Baha'i's status at the court, his intimacy with the king, and his being part of the clerical establishment of Isfahan reflects only one facet of this complex individual. He was known to have donned, at times, the clothing of a dervish and appears in Nurbakhshi and Ni'matallahi Sufi genealogies, indicating that, despite Shah 'Abbas's efforts, Sufi impulses survived even into the Isfahan phase.

Shaykh Baha'i was extremely prolific, having written more than a hundred works on a broad variety of topics, from science to poetry, from literary anthologies to the occult. While it would be incorrect to portray him as too starkly or solely "legalistic," the *Jami'-i 'Abbasi* was his most famous work, and it contributed to the popularization of legalistic Shi'ism. Shaykh Baha'i tells us that Shah 'Abbas commissioned him to write this book so that all the people, including Shi'is and *ghulams*, would be familiar with Shi'i religious necessities, and furthermore, the king ordered that it be written in a clear and understandable way so that everyone could benefit from it. Shaykh Baha'i divided the book into twenty chapters covering a diverse array of topics such as ablutions, supplications (*namaz*), tithing, fasting, pilgrimage, marriage and divorce, compensating victims of injuries, hunting, slaughtering of animals and what is permissible and forbidden, and eating and drinking. That Shah 'Abbas commissioned a work like this also suggests that he was trying to create a clear distinction between the Shi'i practices of his empire and the official Sunnism of the Ottomans.

THE FRIDAY PRAYER CONTROVERSY

One of the topics that Shaykh Baha'i addressed in the *Jami'-i 'Abbasi* was the Friday prayer, which emerged as one of the most extensively debated religious issues of his time: the permissibility of conducting the Friday congregational prayer (*juma'*) in the absence of the Twelfth Imam. The controversy is important because it highlights tensions related to the power and authority held by Shah 'Abbas versus that of the Shi'i theologians. The traditional Friday congregational prayer had been part of the fabric of Sunni Islamic religious expression for centuries. It included a call to prayer, a sermon, or *khutba*, in which the name of the ruler was mentioned, and prayer. But the Shi'i perspective on the practice differed. While Shi'i theologians had made some provisions for participation in the Friday prayers, in general the ritual was discouraged, because the Imams were considered the only legitimate individuals to conduct the services. Anyone else, therefore, was seen as a usurper of the authority of the Imams. After the death of the last Imam, the situation became further complicated because the Imam was no longer alive to designate someone else to conduct the prayer service. Shi'i scholars could not reach consensus on the matter, as some stated Friday prayers were permissible and others stated they were not.

During the reigns of Shah Isma'il and Shah Tahmasb, various Shi'i scholars weighed in on the Friday prayer debate. Shah Isma'il wanted to institute the Friday prayer as a means of consolidating both his rule and Shi'ism in Iran. Al-Karaki, the 'Amili scholar and foremost religious expert at that time, stated that the Friday prayer was not required but permissible as long as it was carried out by a qualified *mujtahid* who would be appointed by a senior cleric. Theoretically, this opinion gave the clerics a great deal of power independent of the sovereign. However, as important a figure as al-Karaki was, his fellow clerics did not agree with his position, and for this reason, the Friday prayer was not really practiced during the time of Shah Isma'il or the first two decades following his death. During the reign of Shah Tahmasb, a spectrum of opinions emerged over its permissibility that reflected the differing views of Shi'i theologians of earlier centuries: some said it was optional, others, required, and still others, not allowed at all. There was also disagreement over whether or not a jurist needed to sanction the prayers. Ultimately, Husayn ibn 'Abd al-Samad (d. 984/1576), Shaykh Baha'i's father, said that the Friday prayers were obligatory and that a jurist was not required to sanction them. As a result of this, Friday prayers were established in some cities in Iran.

The Friday prayer debate did not reach resolution until the time of Shah 'Abbas. The best evidence indicating that the matter had been settled was the building of the Royal Mosque, described in chapter 3, where congregational prayers were held. In addition to this, both Shaykh Baha'i, in his *Jami'-i 'Abbasi*, and the great religious scholar Mir Damad made the Friday prayer permissible but not necessary.

A third religious scholar, Lutf Allah al-Maysi, known as Shaykh Lutf Allah, after whom the Shaykh Lutf Allah Mosque on the royal square in Isfahan was named, went so far as to say that the Friday prayer was obligatory, not optional, and he performed the Friday prayer in his mosque. This perspective, however, did not enjoy wide support. Shaykh Lutf Allah was another 'Amili scholar who became the Shaykh al-Islam of Isfahan. He greatly supported the Safavid state and enjoyed the full backing of the king – Shah 'Abbas even married his daughter. This support came at a price, however. Shaykh Lutf Allah ran into conflicts with a group of merchants who were associated with the old square and the old congregational mosque of

Isfahan. One of these individuals, a guildsman, went to "the court of a few sayyids and notables" and accused Shaykh Lutf Allah of "abrogating sacred law, committing an innovation, and fabricating sources in a number of religious practices" (Abisaab, *Converting*, 83–84). The source of this disagreement probably had its roots in the fact that the new square eclipsed the economic power of the old one and those merchants and guildsmen associated with it lost power and prestige.

THE SCHOOL OF ISFAHAN

In the same way that Shaykh Baha'i's writings went beyond the legalistic to encompass a number of other areas of inquiry, so too did the scholarly output of two of Shaykh Baha'i's contemporaries – Mir Damad (d. 1631) and Mulla Sadra – similarly reflect a broad range of interests. Indeed, they helped elaborate a philosophy that came to be known later by several names including the "Illuminationist (Ishraqi) school" of philosophy and the "School of Isfahan." Shah 'Abbas at the very least tacitly approved of this intellectual activity. He commissioned scholars associated with this "school" to write specific texts, and they dedicated certain of their treatises to the king. He would have realized that the movement provided Safavid Shi'ism with an intellectual depth and maturity that could compete with the Sunni Ottomans and Mughals.

Sayyid Muhammad Baqir Astarabadi was known as Mir Damad. Damad means "son-in-law," and he inherited this title because his father was the son-in-law of al-Karaki, that first influential 'Amili scholar who came to Iran during the reign of Shah Isma'il. Mir Damad was born in Iran, in the city of Astarabad. He studied with a number of scholars, including Shaykh Baha'i's father, Shaykh Husayn ibn 'Abd al-Samad al-'Amili, and was a close associate of Shaykh Baha'i himself.

Mir Damad was, like Shaykh Baha'i, highly prolific, and wrote on topics in philosophy and theology. He also composed his own poetry under the pen name of "Ishraq," an indirect reference to the philosophy of the medieval writer Suhravardi (1154–1191), founder of a school of philosophy known as *hikmat al-ishraq* (philosophy of illuminationism). Suhravardi's ideas offered a critique of Aristotle's scientific methodology, which he believed contained inconsistencies and ambiguities. He argued against the universality of scientific knowledge and "establishes future contingency ... as a scientific principle" (*EI2*, "Suhrawardi"). As a result of his philosophical writings, Mir Damad came to be known as the "third philosopher," after Aristotle and al-Farabi.

Mir Damad's prose was notoriously dense and difficult to read. Abisaab has suggested that he employed this style deliberately, not wanting his ideas to be understood broadly, and more importantly, because he hoped for the king's approval (Abisaab, *Converting*, 75). Shah 'Abbas himself did not oppose Mir Damad's philosophical inquiries – perhaps he did not understand them himself – and indeed, he commissioned Mir Damad to write at least one work, *Al-Jadawat*, in response to questions posed by Indian scholars. These scholars asked why Moses was not consumed in the fire of the Burning Bush, through which God appeared to him. In this Persian treatise, Mir Damad relates the question to larger issues of time, creation, essence, and existence, and God's relationship to all of these. Mir Damad also dedicated to Shah 'Abbas his *Al-Sirat al-mustaqim* (the straight path), in which he discusses "the relationship between the eternal and the created (*EIR*, "Damad")." One of Mir Damad's most important works, the *Kitab-i qabasat*, or the "Book of Fiery Sparks," elaborates and modifies Avicenna's ideas about the relationships between God, creation, and the universe. In addition to Suhravardi, Mir Damad, like many of his contemporaries, drew heavily on the writings of Plato, Aristotle, and Avicenna, adding to them elements of Shi'i thought, all of which reflects the multifaceted nature of the philosophical discourse of this time.

Mir Damad's most prominent student was Sadr al-Din Shirazi, who also studied with Shaykh Baha'i. Known as Mulla Sadra, he spent most of his life teaching and writing in Shiraz. He developed new aspects of the "School of Isfahan," yet at the same time incorporated older strands of thought from the important medieval thinkers such as Avicenna, Ibn al-Arabi, and Suhravardi. He also incorporated ideas from Isma'ili Shi'ism and elsewhere. The result of this synthesis was a philosophy sometimes referred to today as "transcendent wisdom" or "transcendent theosophy." Mulla Sadra wrote on a wide range of topics including mysticism, scriptural commentary, and theology. His best known work, *al-Asfar al-arba'a*, or *The Four Journeys*, follows the journey of the soul through its relationship with God.

SHAH 'ABBAS AND CHRISTIANITY

Shah 'Abbas did not confine his encounters with clerics to just Shi'is. Considerable numbers of Christians, adherents of Eastern Christian churches, such as the Armenians and the Georgians, came to Iran as a result of Safavid territorial expansion and population transfers. Many of these people did not recognize the authority of the pope in Rome and thus had differences in outlook with the Christian missionaries, both Catholic and Protestant, who came to Iran from Europe, often as part of diplomatic embassies or as devotees hopeful of converting Shah 'Abbas.

Isfahan at this time was home to three major Catholic missions: the Augustinian, the Carmelite, and the Capuchin. These groups interacted with each other and with the recently founded Armenian community in New Julfa. For the most part, Shah 'Abbas treated these missionaries with cordial hospitality, though at times he played off one group against the other. Part of his interest in the missionaries and their interest in him related to the mutual hope of establishing a Safavid–European anti-Ottoman alliance. This issue, which will be discussed in greater detail in chapter 5, played a part in shaping the way Shah 'Abbas treated the European Christians in his kingdom. Furthermore, while the missionaries in Iran were not particularly significant in terms of their numbers or influence, their presence resulted in the surfacing of differences between the various Christian factions in Iran, and led to the Shi'i clerical production of anti-Christian polemical treatises.

One example of the kind of conflict that emerged between local Christian populations and European missionaries, and the way Shah 'Abbas became involved with them, can be seen in relations between the Augustinian and the Armenian communities. In 1602, the Catholic Augustinians, who came to Iran as political representatives of Spain and Portugal, had set up a mission in Isfahan with Shah 'Abbas's approval and financial support.

Once established in Isfahan, the Augustinians met with their Armenian counterparts from New Julfa and attempted to persuade the Armenian patriarch David IV to accept the authority of the pope in Rome. In 1607, after many meetings and discussions with the Augustinian leader Diogo de Santa Ana, the patriarch signed a letter of obedience in which he agreed to submit to the pope, and he had a number of his bishops and priests sign the letter with him. He would have had various reasons to do this, ranging from economic incentives promised by the Augustinians, to being recognized as leader of the Armenian church, even though he would be under papal authority. David IV sent a second letter of obedience to the pope, asking for material support and requesting that the pope ask Shah 'Abbas to ensure that the Armenians remain free to worship as they pleased. However, Julfan Armenian clerics had various doctrinal objections to uniting with Rome. There was some concern, for example, over whether or not the Armenians would be able to worship in their own way if they united with Rome. A number of important Julfan merchants, too, were unhappy that David signed the letter at all. Ultimately, the Armenian patriarch retracted his letter of obedience to the pope.

Unhappy about how the events were developing, the Augustinians met with Shah 'Abbas to ask him to persuade the Armenians to join the Catholic church. Initially, Shah 'Abbas agreed to do so and, to the astonishment of the Augustinians, even said he would order the Armenians to comply. However, soon after this, Shah 'Abbas changed his position when he learned that the Holy Roman

Habsburg Emperor Rudolf II and Ahmet I, the Ottoman sultan, had signed the peace treaty of Zsitvatorok. Shah ʻAbbas felt betrayed by this, as it was a clear signal that the Safavid–European alliance against the Ottomans, which the European rulers had seemed to advocate in their letters to Shah ʻAbbas, would not materialize. He reprimanded the Augustinians and ultimately the attempt to unite the Armenians of New Julfa with the Catholic church failed. Shah ʻAbbas's response shows how prevailing political events could alter his decisions.

This political context also helps explain why Shiʻi clerics composed a number of political treatises against Christianity and Judaism. During this time, Shah ʻAbbas was removing the Portuguese from the Persian Gulf region and destroying their fortress on the island of Hormuz. As relations between Shah ʻAbbas and the Portuguese were worsening, Shah ʻAbbas attempted to convert both the residents of Hormuz and the Armenians to Islam. Shah ʻAbbas thus himself commissioned a number of these anti-Christian works.

One of the individuals most involved in this project was Mir Sayyid Ahmad Alavi ʻAmili (d. ca. 1644–1650), known as Ahmad Alavi. Alavi was a student of Mir Damad's, and also his cousin and son-in-law. He dedicated at least one of his compositions – a commentary on two expositions on the writings of the medieval Shiʻi scholar Nasir al-Din Tusi – to Shah ʻAbbas. Alavi had expertise in the Hebrew Bible, which he displayed by quoting Hebrew written in Arabic script, and he also showed great familiarity with the New Testament. Alavi wrote a treatise in response to a Christian polemic that the Jesuit Jerome Xavier had composed in India for the Mughal emperor Jahangir. Originally in Portuguese, Xavier's treatise was translated into Spanish and Persian. In one of his works, Alavi denied the authenticity of the Bible and the prophethood of Jesus. Thus, as Abisaab has noted, with Alavi's treatises we see how Shah ʻAbbas used the clerics in his midst to engage in intellectual warfare and support his political agenda against the Portuguese (Abisaab, *Converting*, 79–81).

Shah 'Abbas's interest in Christianity was not limited to encouraging clerics to write polemics against it. While negotiating relationships between the various religious representatives in his kingdom and often playing the different parties against each other, at the same time it seems that he took a genuine interest in discussing a broad range of religious subjects with his guests. In 1621, some fourteen years after the first Carmelite mission to Iran, Father Vincent of St Francis returned to see the king. He met Shah 'Abbas in Isfahan within the private quarters of the palace. There, the king sat on the floor dining with several other individuals, including one English "agent," or head merchant, his Lutheran chaplain, and four interpreters. The English were there to present the king with gifts. Shah 'Abbas apparently viewed this visit as an opportunity to engage the English and Father Vincent in a religious debate or dialogue, because two days prior, he had a meeting with the English in which they criticized Catholicism. As a result of this encounter, Shah 'Abbas decided to bring Father Vincent and his companion together with the English representatives in order to learn about the differences between Protestantism and Catholicism.

In wide-ranging discussions covering topics such as the papacy, free will, and the Christian cross, Shah 'Abbas's religious sympathies were more with his Catholic guests than with the English Protestants, although in at least one instance his own Islamic background caused him to side with neither party. He agreed with the Catholics when they characterized the "English" (i.e. the Protestant) belief that fasting was not a divine command as an "absurd falsehood and error," and concurred that such a belief was a "very great error and falsehood, because fasts, prayer, penitential exercises and good works are recommended in the law of Moses, in the Gospel, and the Quran, and in fine by all the prophets" (*Carmelites* I, 250).

Regarding free will, Shah 'Abbas also sympathized with the Catholic Carmelites and became particularly outraged when the Fathers told him that the English denied the notion of free will. Of course, this may have been because the Fathers cleverly compared the Protestant position to the beliefs of "the Turks" (the Ottomans). The Carmelites told him that

> the English are heretics and of a like sect as the Turks, who deny free will and say that all the evil men do and the demons do is done of necessity, and they cannot do less, because God so wills: and so they (the English) say that God does everything whether good or evil.

This statement caused the king to launch into a "sermon," speaking with "great gusto" and putting forth numerous arguments against the English position (*Carmelites* I, 251).

When discussing the age of the papacy and the Catholic religion, Shah 'Abbas again sided with the Catholics. The king appears to have taken this position after learning that prior to the split in the church, the English had acknowledged the authority of the pope. Perhaps taking his cue from the analogy that the Fathers had made earlier between English Christianity and Ottoman Sunnism, Shah 'Abbas stated, "just as the Sunnis and Turkish heretics will not ascribe the primacy to Husain ... but instead to 'Umar, so the English do not obey the vicar of Jesus, who is the Pope of Rome: and for this they are heretics" (*Carmelites* I, 252).

Shah 'Abbas disagreed with both Catholic and Protestant beliefs when they came to the topic of the crucifixion of Jesus. Here, he repeated the commonly held Islamic belief that Jesus was not really crucified:

> We hold that the Lord Jesus is the Spirit of God and was not crucified by the Jews, but that God, seeing that the Jews wanted to crucify him, drew him up as the Spirit into heaven, putting the features of Jesus on Judas, who had sold him and whom, because he appeared to be so like Him, they took and crucified.
>
> (*Carmelites* I, 251)

Shah 'Abbas did not confine his interest in Christianity to palace walls or rarified meetings with small groups of religious leaders. In public, he freely interacted with members of the Christian communities that were living in Isfahan and elsewhere, probably for economic reasons. For example, Shah 'Abbas appeared genuinely interested in learning about the Augustinians and their beliefs; he visited their church for the first time in 1608, showing respect to the icons of Jesus and Mary therein, and went to the church on Christmas day, even ensuring that the Augustinians would have pork to eat and wine to drink for their holiday, much to the chagrin of the clerics in his entourage.

In another instance, Shah 'Abbas attended an Armenian religious ceremony in which crosses were taken and dipped into the Zayandah river in Isfahan. In this very public ritual, Armenians and other people from Isfahan gathered on the banks to watch. When Shah 'Abbas and the Armenian patriarch reached a small "islet" in the center of the river from which the service would be staged, the king became restless and proceeded to act as master of ceremonies for the entire ceremony, directing participants where to stand and what to do. After the event had finished, he spent the rest of the day and the night at the home of the "principal Armenian," Khvajah Safar, where he discussed religious matters and then asked to see some of their relics. Shah 'Abbas's reverence for the relics and the respect he showed them, including kissing them and holding them over his head, came as a great surprise to those who were present (*Carmelites* I, 245).

On the same day or evening, Shah 'Abbas decided to gift a portion of an Armenian relic – a bone allegedly from the body of Rhipsima (d. ca. 290), an early female Armenian saint and martyr – to one of the Carmelite Fathers. Della Valle describes the scene as follows:

> Even more astonishing – in a Muslim monarch, and that the Armenian clergy tolerated it with such equanimity, for the two Augustinian friars present were scandalized – was that the Shah took it into his head that he would make a gift of a piece of the relic of S. Ripsima, the famed virgin and martyr of Armenia, to Fr. John Thaddeus, and not only touched but broke the bone of the Saint with his own hands and, wrapping it in a piece of clean paper, handed it to the Carmelite Vicar Provincial.
>
> (*Carmelites* I, 245–246)

RELIGION AND KINGSHIP

In terms of his personal religiosity, Shah 'Abbas was a master of public displays of religious devotion, as seen in his numerous pilgrimages to Mashhad and to Ardabil. This image carried into print as well: one of his court chroniclers, the astrologer Munajjim Yazdi, consistently refers to him as the "dog of the threshold of 'Ali." Dogs were often seen as symbols of humility in Persian literature, and in this way, Yazdi promoted the notion that Shah 'Abbas held a highly subservient position in relation to the first Imam. When it came to religious law, however, Shah 'Abbas's relationship to Islamic and Shi'i normative practices was more complex. For example, recent research has shown that in the case of the partaking of alcohol, which was generally forbidden under Islamic law, Shah 'Abbas went through various phases of both banning and allowing alcohol in his empire. On one occasion in 1603, during a campaign against the Qizilbash, wine was banned on pain of death (Matthee, *Pursuit*, 81).

On other occasions, however, the king appears to have enjoyed drinking wine and held gatherings in which he invited travelers and visitors to Iran to partake of alcohol. Indeed, activities such as merry-making (which included drinking), hunting, and fighting in battle were all important aspects of traditional Persian kingship in which Shah 'Abbas actively and enthusiastically participated. According to a broad range of primary sources, Shah 'Abbas's parties "were merry gatherings that never seem to have degenerated into drunken orgies" (Matthee, *Pursuit*, 52). When Pietro Della Valle met Shah 'Abbas at a royal gathering, the king welcomed him and ordered that wine be served. Della Valle, however, complained about the wine, saying that it was "neither very strong nor very good." Although the entertainment at that gathering continued until past 1:00 A.M., Shah 'Abbas was "all the time conducting himself with great familiarity, yet constantly preserving his dignity" (Della Valle, 229–234/64–65). Perhaps to legitimize such behavior, he had his personal physician compose a treatise on the advantages of drinking alcohol.

Courtly entertainment also included music, singing, and dancing. Della Valle describes an elderly female singer at the court named Filfil (Pepper) who was occasionally hired, despite her age, "to divert company," and was treated well, "merely on account of her being one of those who occasionally appeared before the King" (Della Valle, 20–21/19). The king's partaking of alcohol and hosting entertainment at his court made a public statement that he was above the law. As Matthee has stated,

> The king was not just allowed to drink; he was supposed to drink, both as a sign of his status and stature as a 'big man,' and as a demonstration that, as the descendant of the sinless Imam, he was beyond the strictures of Islam, occupied his own autonomous moral space and thus personified the body politic.
>
> (Matthee, *Pursuit*, 67)

During the Isfahan phase of his rule, Shah 'Abbas was able to use religion for political ends, whether undertaking a pilgrimage to Mashhad on foot, maintaining control over the powerful clerics, or interacting with Christians. His apparent ease in dealing with a wide range of people also worked to his advantage in the areas of warfare and diplomacy, as will be seen in the following chapter.

5

FROM HALF THE WORLD TO THE OTHER HALF: WARFARE AND DIPLOMACY

The establishment of Isfahan and the consolidation of his rule, which included close supervision of the clerics, allowed Shah 'Abbas finally to address the external challenges that had shadowed him since he became king. After moving the capital to Isfahan, he fought and won two major wars, one against the Uzbeks and one against the Ottomans. At the same time, Shah 'Abbas's relations with peoples beyond the borders of his empire were not confined to military conflict; indeed, the openness with which he treated travelers and visitors – who came to Isfahan with either commercial, religious, diplomatic, or other motives – stands out as a striking feature of his reign. Like none of his Safavid predecessors, he made Iran a significant player on the world stage. Here we shall consider the following themes and events under the broad category of warfare and diplomacy: (1) the Khurasan campaign against the Uzbeks, (2) Shah 'Abbas's diplomatic relations with Europe, and (3) the campaigns against the Ottomans.

Because it was the first war that he fought after transferring the capital to Isfahan and consolidating power internally, the Khurasan campaign was very important, both militarily and politically, to Shah 'Abbas. For this reason, an in-depth examination of this campaign, preceded by an overview of Safavid firearm usage, will allow us a better understanding of the nature of warfare and its relationship to politics and kingship during Shah 'Abbas's reign.

FIREARMS

Shah 'Abbas ruled over the Safavids at a time when gunpowder and firearms were being used not only in his empire, but also by the neighboring Ottomans, Mughals, and Uzbeks. He utilized firearms along with his new *ghulam* forces in the conquest of Khurasan against the Uzbeks. Until fairly recently, a myth persisted that the Safavids did not use firearm technology until the brothers Anthony and Robert Sherley journeyed to Iran from England and brought it to Shah 'Abbas's attention. This assumption is incorrect. It is true that in the early Safavid period, the Ottoman Sultan Selim defeated Shah Isma'il and his Safavid army at the Battle of Chaldiran in 1514 because the Ottomans employed firearms and the Safavids did not. But after this happened, Shah Isma'il set about making changes. He asked Venice for assistance in the form of cannon and military expertise, and established a corps of artillerymen (*tupchi*) and musketeers (*tufangchi*) in his army, appointing a rifleman commander (*tufangchi-bashi*) to lead it. The size of this military unit expanded over time, such that by the mid-sixteenth century, it numbered anywhere between 8,000 and 12,000 musketeers. Shah Isma'il was not even the first ruler of Iran to use firearms; it is likely that the practice predated the Safavids and such weaponry was probably used by the pre-Safavid Turkoman dynasty, the Aq Qoyunlu.

By Shah 'Abbas's time, the Safavids were using two types of guns, matchlock and fireflint, and cannons of various sizes, some capable of shooting balls weighing up to ninety pounds. It was also during Shah 'Abbas's reign that we see the Safavids employing, for the first time, a swivel gun known as the "little bee" (*zanburak*), which was set on a camel's back and fired when the camel was either kneeling or running. The Safavids became so competent in cannon construction that by the late sixteenth century they were able to produce them on the spot. Since sulfur, nitrate, and saltpeter – all ingredients used in producing gunpowder – were available in places such as Azerbaijan and Natanz, the Safavids were able to produce at least some guns and gunpowder within their own borders. Despite this, Shah 'Abbas still went to considerable effort to obtain firearms from Europe. He sent embassies to Russia and Venice that came back with firearms in 1595 and 1613, respectively, and England sent him guns in 1618 and 1621, including some 1500 arquebuses.

The biggest problem that the Safavids seemed to face regarding firearms was not obtaining them, but incorporating them into their existing military traditions and practices. As the Safavid army was largely on horseback, firearms slowed the army down in terms of their weight and bulk. Furthermore, they created a loud noise, and their use required a soldier on horseback to dismount, which was seen as undignified. The individuals who were charged with employing firearms were not the most elite elements in the army. Indeed, they were often peasants and laborers, and were viewed with disdain by the mounted cavalry. Thus, while Shah 'Abbas's army had access to firearms produced at home, and the king himself was keen on acquiring them from abroad, the extent of their actual use on the battlefield was rather minimal. The Safavids had better success with cannon, which they used to good effect in sieges, such as their attack on Tabriz in 1585.

THE BATTLE FOR KHURASAN: SHAH 'ABBAS AND THE UZBEKS

The Uzbeks, situated on Iran's eastern border, were the dominant power in Central Asia, where they ruled over Transoxiana as "khans," or descendants of the famous world conqueror Chingis (Genghis) Khan via his son Jochi and grandson Shiban. For this reason, they are sometimes referred to as Shibanids, or Shibani Uzbeks. Conflicts between the Safavids and Uzbeks had begun in 1506, only five years after the establishment of the Safavid state. In the same way that Qandahar was the major point of conflict between Mughals and Safavids, so too did Herat become the primary focus of the clash between Uzbeks and Safavids. One year prior to Shah 'Abbas's coronation, in 1587, the Uzbeks had launched a campaign in Khurasan whereby they took control of the city of Herat away from the Safavids. After this victory, the Uzbeks went on to expand their power towards the northwest and west. In a particularly humiliating defeat for Shah 'Abbas, the Uzbek leader 'Abd al-Mu'min Khan took Mashhad in 1589.

NARRATING THE CAMPAIGN

Nearly ten years after he signed the embarrassing treaty with the Ottomans and executed Ya'qub Khan, Shah 'Abbas was finally in a position to address the Uzbek threat and re-capture Herat. On 9 April 1598, Shah 'Abbas left Isfahan, only a month or so after he moved the capital there, on a decisive campaign to Khurasan. The Safavid chroniclers, after having to justify and explain years of defeat, could now turn to narrating a Safavid victory, and they seem to have taken special pleasure in doing so, particularly Siyaqi Nizam, whose chronicle was devoted entirely to the Khurasan campaign. Several factors help explain the emphasis on this episode, which, in addition to its military significance, also had religious and political import. In the same way that the elimination of Ya'qub Khan represented Shah 'Abbas's triumph against the Qizilbash, the Khurasan campaign signaled a turning point against external threats.

THE BATTLE AGAINST THE UZBEKS

Shah 'Abbas appointed the Georgian *ghulam* Allahverdi Khan to head the expedition. A key figure in the Khurasan campaign, Allahverdi Khan served as both commander of the *ghulams* (*qullar aqasi*) and commander-in-chief (*amir al-ulama*) of Fars and Khuzestan.

Allahverdi Khan led the entire left wing of the Safavid army, which was composed of *ghulam* forces, while Husayn Khan Qajar headed the Shamlu and other amirs in the right wing.

Shah 'Abbas made an important stop in Mashhad on his way to meet up with Allahverdi Khan, who had taken a different route to Khurasan. His stay there shows how he combined military objectives with displays of public piety in order to advance his political agenda. The chronicler Siyaqi Nizam notes Shah 'Abbas's devotion and at the same time emphasizes his divine assurance of ultimate military success:

> He dismounted along with the amirs and the nobles and the intimates of the court and began to circumambulate that brightly lit tomb [of Imam Reza]. He traversed the path of servitude with the steps of true faith, and a flood of tears of supplication rushed upon his sun-like face from his jewel like eyes … and from the denizens of the concourse on high he heard the call, "whosoever enters therein is safe," [Q. 3:96] and in the dust of that lofty threshold he beheld the countenance of triumph and victory from behind the invisible veil.
>
> (Siyaqi Nizam, *Fotuhat*, 376)

Shah 'Abbas also made a point of displaying humility at the shrine, as he swept the carpets and spent three days in prayer there.

One of Shah 'Abbas's greatest military skills was his ability to strategize effectively, and he displayed this talent upon leaving Mashhad. Prior to his departure from the city, the king learned that the Uzbek leader 'Abd al-Mu'min Khan had died. He determined that the Uzbeks would be far easier to defeat if their new leader, Din Muhammad Khan, and his army were unaware that the shah was with his troops. The king received intelligence that Din Muhammad Khan had gathered an army of anywhere between 14,000 and 40,000 men – the sources are not in agreement on this – ready for war and knew that the Safavid vanguard had already set out, but was unaware that Shah 'Abbas had accompanied his army. Had they known this fact, the king believed, war would be prolonged and more difficult because the Uzbeks would retreat into the fortress of Herat and the Safavid army would presumably have a more difficult time attacking the Uzbeks in the fortress than in the open battlefield.

Taking all of this into consideration, Shah 'Abbas then employed a strategy that Shah Isma'il had used to good advantage: he planned to spread a rumor among the Uzbeks that he had to leave the area for Iraq and/or Azerbaijan in order to deal with a new Ottoman threat. After broadcasting that rumor, Shah 'Abbas headed for Herat and met up with Allahverdi Khan on the Herat river. Falling for the ruse, Din Muhammad Khan came out of his fortress in Herat and was obliged to fight the Safavids in a pitched battle, when Shah 'Abbas caught up with him. This was something the Uzbeks did not like to do, because their preferred mode of fighting was to lure their enemy across the Oxus and force them into pursuit. Then they would attack the countryside and Safavid garrisons in the urban areas.

The Safavid and Uzbek armies, with 10,000 and 12,000 soldiers, respectively, fought a pitched battle at Rabat-i Pariyan, near Herat. Shah 'Abbas's army wounded Din Muhammad Khan, causing the Uzbeks to retreat with the Safavids rapidly following them. Ultimately, the Safavids enjoyed a decisive victory; one chronicler notes that in addition to Din Muhammad Khan himself, Safavid forces killed or captured more than 5000 Uzbeks, including a number of notable Uzbek leaders, among them the governors of the important cities of Herat, Mashhad, Nisa, and Abivard.

A significant casualty of the campaign against the Uzbeks was the Qizilbash Farhad Khan Qaramanlu. His fate reflects, as Matthee notes, the transformations that Shah 'Abbas was imposing on Safavid society at the time, where *ghulams* were replacing Qizilbash (*EIR*, "Farhad Khan Qaramanlu"). Farhad Khan had earlier headed a successful expedition to the Caspian provinces, and gradually became extremely powerful, controlling a great deal of territory. The sources are not entirely clear what happened to him during the campaign, but it seems that he became too powerful for his own good. Ultimately Shah 'Abbas had him executed and replaced by Allahverdi Khan, and the land that Farhad Khan had controlled became part of crown land.

As a result of the Khurasan campaign, the Safavids regained control of Herat and Mashhad, and added Balkh, Marv, and Astarabad to their holdings. That this triumph was re-enacted in the royal square of Isfahan as described in chapter 3 above indicates the significance that this victory held for the king. Shah 'Abbas could now start engaging in diplomacy with various European powers and thinking about how to improve his position in relation to the Ottomans.

SHAH 'ABBAS'S EUROPEAN DIPLOMACY

Europe at the time of Shah 'Abbas was well into its age of exploration. The most important maritime power until the late sixteenth century was Portugal, which had set up trading posts in the Indian Ocean so that passing ships would have to stop and pay customs duties. Eventually, however, the Portuguese entered competition with the Dutch and the English, who set up their own rival trading networks and eclipsed the Portuguese. The Dutch and the English became successful because they established privately funded trading companies that enjoyed government support, but they were not government-owned. The EIC, or English East India Company, established in 1600, and the Dutch Company, the VOC or Vereenigde Oostindische Compagnie, established in 1602, clashed occasionally as they vied with each other economically.

Politically, Europe was divided and developing as independent states rather than large empires. By the time of Shah 'Abbas, the Holy Roman Empire had broken up, and its vast holdings, following the 1556 abdication of the Habsburg emperor Charles V, were divided up. Charles V's grandson, King Philip III of Spain, inherited Spain, Italy, and the Low Countries (which later became Belgium and the Netherlands) from his father King Philip II, and Charles V's grandson Rudolf II inherited Austria and the title of Holy Roman Emperor. The Holy Roman Empire had never been able to take over all of Europe due to various rival powers, including the Ottomans, aligning with each other in order to prevent it from expanding too much. Religiously, Europe was also disunited. In the aftermath of the Protestant Reformations, conflicts broke out along sectarian lines, culminating in the Thirty Years War that began in 1618.

As Shah 'Abbas entered into diplomatic relations with various European powers, two main issues dominated the messages that ambassadors, diplomats, religious figures, and envoys relayed back and forth between Shah 'Abbas and Europe: (1) the desire to establish a European–Safavid alliance against the Ottomans, and (2) the desire to divert the silk trade from an overland east–west route that went through Ottoman territory to a north–south route that went by sea. Given the fractured state of Europe, many obstacles thwarted these efforts, including communication problems: it sometimes took several years for a letter to reach its intended recipient, and by the time such a letter did arrive, the political reality had changed to such a degree that it rendered the message obsolete. Furthermore, messages did not always arrive in the order in which they were sent, and envoys sometimes crossed paths. Despite the political impasses and failures to forge alliances, as a result of the exchanges, the Safavids and the various European powers became increasingly familiar with each other, as more and more individuals traveled between Iran and Europe, to the extent that, for example, Shakespeare made reference to "the Sophy" – an Anglicized version of "Safavi" – in his play *Twelfth Night*. At the same time, the Safavids were becoming more familiar with European styles and fashions. Such familiarity made its way into areas of Safavid artistic expression such as painting, as we will discuss in chapter 6.

THE ANTI-OTTOMAN ALLIANCE

While attempts on the part of European powers to engage Iran in an anti-Ottoman alliance went back to the period of Shah Isma'il, it was not until Shah 'Abbas's reign that diplomacy surrounding this issue took place on a regular basis. The first and perhaps best known Europeans who visited Iran during Shah 'Abbas's reign were an Englishman and his brother. In 1598, at the apparent bidding of the Earl of Essex, Sir Anthony Sherley and his brother, Sir Robert Sherley, traveled to Qazvin with a party of some twenty-five people. They arrived in Qazvin in early December 1598, some nine months after Shah 'Abbas had already moved the capital to Isfahan and was away on his Uzbek campaign. Soon after the Sherleys' arrival, however, Shah 'Abbas marched proudly and triumphantly back to Qazvin after his victory against the Uzbeks and met the brothers there.

After a brief stay in Qazvin, Shah 'Abbas took the Sherleys and their entourage to Isfahan with him. The brothers, colorful characters in early modern British and Iranian history, came to Iran for adventure and fortune and in pursuit of two aims: first, to create a European–Safavid alliance against the Ottomans, and second, to promote trade between Persia and England. Shah 'Abbas treated both brothers, especially Anthony Sherley, with much hospitality and paid them a great deal of attention. While he consistently did this with most visitors, the timing of the Sherleys' visit produced excellent publicity for the king as he returned from the Uzbek campaign.

At the time of the Sherleys' arrival in Iran, Shah 'Abbas was interested in gaining support for an alliance against the Ottomans. He therefore sent Anthony Sherley back to Europe along with the Persian ambassador Husayn 'Ali Beg and Nicolao de Melo, a Portuguese Augustinian, in late April/early May 1599. This was the first of several embassies that Shah 'Abbas sent to various European powers with similar objectives.

Anthony Sherley took with him "letters of friendship" written by Shah 'Abbas to at least nine European leaders, including Queen Elizabeth I and Philip III of Spain. He was able to meet in person with Rudolf II, the Hapsburg Holy Roman Emperor and King of Bohemia, whom he saw in Prague. Upon their arrival in Rome, in

April 1601, things took a turn for the worse within the entourage when Anthony quarreled over precedence with Husayn 'Ali Beg. As a result of the disagreement, in which Husayn 'Ali Beg claimed to be the main ambassador, not Anthony Sherley, they were unable to meet with Pope Clement VIII at the scheduled time. All of this caused Husayn 'Ali Beg to proceed on his own to Spain. Anthony, meanwhile, went to Venice, where he exchanged letters with Philip III of Spain. There, English agents discovered the letters, pronouncing them treasonable. Anthony was subsequently imprisoned, and stayed behind bars from April 1603 until some time later that year.

The rest of the embassy, having proceeded to Spain without Anthony Sherley, experienced challenges of another sort: Husayn 'Ali Beg's nephew, who had accompanied him on the journey, and one of his companions, Uruch Beg, converted to Christianity. The ruler of Spain, King Philip III, adopted them and gave them the Christian names of Felipe and Juan, respectively. Juan, or "Don Juan," mentioned above in chapter 2, went on to write an account of his travels. This left Husayn 'Ali Beg and the entire embassy embarrassed and disgraced, and seeking to punish the converts. Husayn 'Ali Beg even plotted, unsuccessfully, to have his nephew murdered. In terms of the actual results of these embassies, Shah 'Abbas received a number of polite letters containing offers of friendship from the leaders to whom he had sent messages. But despite this courtesy, the European powers were simply not interested enough or sufficiently united to form a specific plan. Ultimately, Shah 'Abbas must have known this was the case, for even before Husayn 'Ali Beg returned from Europe, he decided to resume war with the Ottomans in 1603.

DIVERTING THE FLOW OF SILK

Despite the considerable academic interest in the Sherley brothers, the Iberian powers played the greatest role in the anti-Ottoman strategy and attempts to divert the silk trade. Portuguese missionaries, Augustinians, and Carmelites all became involved in this international game. Considerable diplomacy took place between Europe and Iran over diverting the silk trade away from the traditional Anatolian route and through the Persian Gulf instead. Shah 'Abbas was interested in trade with Europe primarily because he needed the funds to finance his wars and pay his army. At this time, the demand for raw silk in Europe had increased, but the traditional overland trade carried out by the Armenians, with its route through Ottoman territory and ports in the Levant, had suffered from the latest round of Ottoman–Safavid wars. The idea, attractive both to the Europeans and to Shah 'Abbas, who wanted to keep all of his options open, was to redirect the trade away from the Levant ports and instead send the silk via a maritime route. In connection with this effort, Shah 'Abbas was also trying to consolidate his rule over the southern portion of Iran and thus Allahverdi Khan, at the shah's orders, took the province of Lar in 1601 and a year later seized Bahrain, a Portuguese protectorate.

In 1609, Shah 'Abbas sent Antonio de Gouvea, an Augustinian missionary who had come to Iran a year earlier to meet the shah, and Dengiz Beg Rumlu, a Qizilbash ambassador, to Rome and Spain in order to explore the possibility of diverting the silk traffic. Gouvea was an important figure, partly because he spent a great deal of time with Shah 'Abbas, and is an important source of information on the monarch. Gouvea had already been to Iran once before in 1602–1603, having assisted in establishing the Augustinian mission in Isfahan. One of the purposes of his 1608 trip to Iran was to gather intelligence on Shah 'Abbas for King Philip III of Spain (who was also Philip II of Portugal).

On Gouvea's trip back to Europe, he and his party took with them raw silk for Philip III. Among the several points in Shah 'Abbas's letter was the proposal to divert the silk from Iran. The plan would have Philip III purchasing silk from Hormuz, where it would be sent to Europe on Portuguese ships. Gouvea arrived in Spain in 1610, and while the Spanish Council of State accepted the idea of sending ships twice a year to pick up the silk and not pay customs on export goods, the proposal never became an actual policy of the Spanish. More importantly, it is unclear whether or not Shah 'Abbas ever really intended to carry out the plan. Rather, the suggestion has been made that much of this was for show, and that the Armenians, who were active and privileged partners in the silk trade, never would have agreed to such a plan. Ultimately, the entire scheme reflects Shah 'Abbas's outstanding abilities to strategize, as it was "designed to intimidate the Ottomans as much as to manipulate the Europeans" (Matthee, *Politics*, 82).

Shah 'Abbas, or at least his ambassador, made one more attempt to raise the issue of diverting the silk, this time in 1615. Although by now the Safavids had made peace with the Ottomans, the possibility of war breaking out surfaced again. This was because the Ottoman grand vizier who had favored peace with the Safavids had been executed. Shah 'Abbas therefore chose to send Robert Sherley back to Europe. Robert Sherley had remained in Iran when Shah 'Abbas first sent his brother Anthony to Europe, in order to ensure his brother's "good behavior" (Savory, *Iran*, 109). Robert himself had already gone on one ineffective mission to Europe in 1608, but this time he wanted Robert to reach an agreement with the Portuguese regarding their trading presence in Hormuz. Robert Sherley was also unsuccessful in this mission. He returned to Iran some twelve years later, only to find that he was out of favor with the shah. He died in Qazvin in debt in 1627.

Shah 'Abbas also explored a third route for Iran's silk, one that went to Moscow via Astrakhan and the Caspian Sea. Shah 'Abbas's initial interest in the Muscovite state was in forming a joint anti-Ottoman alliance, but he also had a secondary interest in promoting trade. Safavid relations with Moscow had their ups and downs, but the most tangible result of diplomatic embassies between the two states was Shah 'Abbas securing, in 1592, toll-free trade with Moscow for government items. Increasingly, however, Shah 'Abbas became less interested in the anti-Ottoman alliance, and more concerned over Moscow's designs on his northern frontier. Relations with Moscow deteriorated after the Safavids subjugated

Kakheti, in Georgia, in 1605, and did not resume until 1613. By this time, however, Shah ʿAbbas was already pursuing the possibility of trade through the Persian Gulf and showed even less interest in Russia. The two powers did continue to have commercial relations, though, and traded silk in the 1620s.

TRAVELERS TO THE SHAH

Shah ʿAbbas opened Iran's doors to travelers, a number of whom are mentioned in this volume, who entered the country with increasing frequency during his reign. Many such individuals, whether visiting Iran as ambassadors, missionaries, traders, or adventurers, left lasting impressions of their experiences and of Shah ʿAbbas. Some people made their way to Safavid territory for more personal reasons. Pietro Della Valle was said to have gone to Iran to recover from a broken heart and perhaps out of boredom over the ease of his life back in Rome. Della Valle was a bibliophile who sought out Arabic medical and religious manuscripts in the Levant during his early travels. In the aftermath of the Sherleys' trip to Iran, he wanted to meet the Safavid king and offer his services in defeating the Ottomans by forming an alliance with the Cossacks and recapturing the Holy Land. He also wanted to safeguard the Christian communities in the region by situating a colony in Isfahan where Chaldeans and Nestorians could live in safety. Della Valle had numerous adventures on his journeys. It appears he recovered from his broken heart, as he met and married a Nestorian-Armenian woman named Maʿani Juwayri when traveling through Baghdad, but she died shortly after the marriage. Because Della Valle was fluent in Turkish, he could converse with Shah ʿAbbas without a translator, and he left enduring descriptions of his encounters with the king. Della Valle's account of his travels, in the form of eighteen letters and another narrative of his journey, survives as the most significant result of his travels east; like others before him, he was not successful in achieving his other goals.

THE WESTERN FRONT: SHAH 'ABBAS AND THE OTTOMANS

With the Qizilbash threat under control, Isfahan in the process of being established as a strong and central capital city, and Mashhad and Herat in Safavid hands, Shah 'Abbas could now turn to his most formidable external enemy: the Ottomans, at whose hands in 1590 he had been forced to sign an unfavorable treaty giving them territory that had previously been under Safavid control. He was now at last ready to take that land back, despite the lack of any substantial support from the European powers. Shah 'Abbas began his campaigns against the Ottoman empire when he departed from Isfahan on 14 September 1603, setting out to recover the provinces of Azerbaijan and Shirvan. That Shah 'Abbas chose this particular time to mount his offense against the Ottomans testifies to his sense of strategic timing; the Ottomans were at this point already in the midst of fighting on two fronts, externally against the Habsburgs to the west, and at the same time trying to suppress an internal uprising of rebels known as Jalalis in eastern Anatolia. Finally, the Ottoman garrison also had to strike against a rebellious Kurdish local ruler, giving Shah 'Abbas yet another advantage.

Perhaps the most significant, at least politically, of these victories against the Ottomans was the retaking of Tabriz. In the same way that the Uzbek occupation of Mashhad was a source of embarrassment to the Safavids, the Ottoman takeover of Azerbaijan in general and Tabriz in particular had damaged the Safavid image. After all, Tabriz was the first capital city of the Safavid dynasty and the place where Shah Isma'il crowned himself king, established Shi'ism as the official religion, and inaugurated the dynasty. However, even before Shah 'Abbas's military campaign to Azerbaijan, Tabriz had suffered as a result of his policy of diverting the silk traffic away from Tabriz and towards Isfahan.

In the military operation directed against Tabriz, while technologically the Safavids were still using older-style large cannons against superior and smaller Ottoman guns capable of rapid fire,

Shah 'Abbas nevertheless engaged in the Ottoman practice of building fortresses as a way of ensuring that conquered lands would remain in the victor's hands, demonstrating that he could learn from his enemies. While forcing marches upon his troops, at the same time, he was able to keep them motivated through a nine-month campaign, including the winter months.

Following his success in Tabriz, Shah 'Abbas pressed on to other towns in Azerbaijan, bringing Nakhjavan and Yerevan under Safavid rule. It was during the course of this campaign that he ordered the depopulation of Julfa, as described in chapter 3. The campaign in Yerevan was particularly hard on the Safavids, because Yerevan had three well-stocked and well-manned forts that the Safavids found difficult to attack. To make matters worse for the Safavids, those Ottoman soldiers who had been routed from Nakhjavan had fled to Yerevan, bringing the number of Ottoman forces there to 12,000. A long winter siege ensued; the Safavids were unable to dig trenches due to the cold, and the Ottomans did not surrender until June 1604. After Yerevan, Shah 'Abbas defeated the Ottomans in the eastern Anatolian regions of Qars, Erzerum, and Van. He ended the campaign by overtaking Sufiyan, which was just north of Tabriz. All of these were areas that the Ottomans had taken in violation of the 1555 Treaty of Amasya, signed by the Ottomans and Safavids during the reign of Shah Tahmasb.

The campaign against the Ottomans ended some five years after it started, but tensions between the two states continued throughout Shah 'Abbas's reign. The major conflicts included the Safavid destruction of the area from Yerevan to Van in 1613 to prevent an Ottoman attack on Iran, and an unsuccessful Ottoman bid to retake Yerevan in 1616. The two sides attempted to initiate peace talks throughout this period but these efforts did not lead to the signing of another treaty. At best, a sort of stalemate lasted until 1623, when the Safavids took the city of Baghdad, as will be discussed in chapter 7.

Shah 'Abbas was able to accomplish much in the areas of warfare and diplomacy, given the context in which he was operating. Soon after the establishment of Isfahan, he defeated the Uzbeks to the east. He then proceeded to exert a great deal of effort in an attempt to put Iran on the world stage. He received numerous ambassadors, envoys, and travelers at his court, and deftly tried to extract as much political advantage as he could from each encounter. The foreigners who met him found the experience memorable enough that his fame even reached the ears of Shakespeare. Not content simply to receive visitors, he also sent a number of his own embassies to various parts of the world, in order to gain support for an alliance against the Ottomans or to divert the silk trade. While neither of these ventures was particularly successful, he was nevertheless able to defeat the Ottomans without European assistance. Shah 'Abbas's understanding of politics was broad and expansive; it extended beyond the traditional spheres of warfare and diplomacy to the arts, which he enlisted in the service of kingship.

6

THE ARTS IN THE SERVICE OF KINGSHIP

While the city of Isfahan served as a living architectural tribute to the monarch and the most conspicuous display of his kingship, Shah 'Abbas also utilized other forms of artistic expression to project his power and authority. Partly for that reason, the arts thrived during his rule. The two kings before Shah 'Abbas – Isma'il II and Muhammad Khudabanda – did not support the arts in the way that Shah Tahmasb had done in the earlier years of his reign. Thus, it was not until Shah 'Abbas's coming to power that the royal library where artists, painters, and calligraphers engaged in their craft became re-established, and artists who had largely fallen to fending for themselves or working in provincial courts were able to secure employment at the Safavid center. In Isfahan, the influx of European and Chinese art made the capital a cosmopolitan place for artists to work.

Shah 'Abbas showed interest in a broad range of art forms that included but were not limited to calligraphy and painting, textiles, and metal work. He formed close relationships with some of the most prominent artists in his kingdom, and they accompanied him on his travels and military campaigns. Shah 'Abbas's reign also witnessed new developments in traditional art forms and the spread of specific motifs, decorations, and patterns onto multiple forms. Finally, art was used in connection with diplomacy, as various precious objects were sent to and from the Safavid court in order to further political objectives.

This chapter emphasizes the relationship between the king and the arts and artists. It is not a general survey of Safavid art during Shah 'Abbas's reign. Here, we shall briefly examine the new elements in Safavid art during this period and Shah 'Abbas's use of those elements in such a way as to give his empire a new visual identity. We will then explore Shah 'Abbas's relationship with select artists, and end with an overview of the practice of gift-giving in relation to art and kingship, both internationally and domestically.

NEW ARTISTIC STYLES

The reign of Shah 'Abbas witnessed the development of new artistic styles at the court in Isfahan. Such styles can be seen on a wide variety of media, including carpets, books, and portraits. In the area of carpet design and production, as a result of Shah 'Abbas's promotion of and support for the silk production industry, Safavid looms created large numbers of carpets and textiles made with gold and silver thread and which featured new colors. In the gold and silver carpets, artisans wove strands of silver around white silk thread, giving the illusion that the carpet was made of silver. Similarly, wrapping silver around a yellow silk thread made it appear as though the carpet were made of gold. The actual designs on the gold and silver carpets varied; some contained small-scale elements, reminiscent of earlier styles, and others had larger, bold designs, reflecting more current trends. This new style of carpet would have covered the floors of the new mosques on the royal square in Isfahan and elsewhere in the Safavid empire. While gold and silver were the most distinct features of these carpets, they also contained certain colors that were similarly associated with the "new look" of the era. In a group of some 200 surviving carpets, the predominant colors are peach, light green and blue, and beige, with a small amount of dark blue or black.

New styles and decorations also characterized the "arts of the book," which included both bookbinding and illustration.

Illuminated manuscripts were one of the most significant art forms in pre-modern and early modern Iran. Calligraphy and painting went hand in hand to the extent that many Safavid paintings contain within their borders calligraphic inscriptions, and painters and calligraphers worked together in the royal workshops.

The most significant development in miniature painting was the proliferation of single-page illustrations, usually in the form of a portrait or a single sheet of calligraphy that would be mounted on a larger piece of paper and collected into an album. Owners could add, remove, or re-arrange items from the album pages. In this way, artists and calligraphers were able to sell a single page of their art faster than the time it would take them to copy out or illustrate an entire manuscript. Such albums were fashionable both in Iran and in India and popularized the single-page stand-alone miniature painting or calligraphic piece. The royal workshops still produced full-length books, but the books sported new forms of decorations, such as pages embellished with floral sprays and a "jutting lobed form" called a crown (*taj*). New gold "lancelet leaf" forms appeared in between lines of text. On the actual book covers, new colors, consisting of peach, tan, and maroon, replaced the older gold on blue, red, or green paper (Canby, *Shah 'Abbas*, 46, 47, 83).

A NEW VISUAL IDENTITY

The designs and motifs described above were not just unique due to their newness. Certain of these patterns appeared on multiple art forms. Recent scholarship has suggested that Shah 'Abbas promoted this practice deliberately, in order to provide his empire with a "visual identity" or style, set by the royal court. In this way, he used the arts to promote his centralizing policies. For example, the tiles covering the Shaykh Lutf Allah Mosque are decorated with arabesque designs similar to prayer carpets produced during the same period, and lotus blossom motifs on the tiles of the Shaykh Lutf Allah Mosque and the Masjid-i Shah can be seen on silk textiles, illuminated manuscripts, and decorations at the Safavid shrine at Aradabil. A prayer rug, bookbinding, illuminations, and mosque domes all bear the same white "split-palmette" leaves design (Canby, *Shah 'Abbas*, 20). The same color combination of gold and silver seen in the new carpet styles of the era also appears in the illuminations found on manuscript borders, indicating that the same color combinations were popular among artists who worked in various media and forms.

CALLIGRAPHERS AND PAINTERS

The social and political milieu in which artists provided the new visual imprint for the Safavid empire was full of intrigue, gossip, jealousy, and difficult personalities. Shah 'Abbas himself maintained close connections to individual artists, especially calligraphers and painters. While many artists and artisans produced pieces of stunning beauty, decorating and embellishing both paper and buildings, space allows us only to mention a few of those individuals who had significant interactions with Shah 'Abbas. Four figures numbered among the most prominent calligraphers and painters of the period and the artists that Shah 'Abbas admired most. These were (1) Sadiqi Beg Afshar, one of Shah 'Abbas's favorite painters, (2) the calligrapher 'Ali Riza 'Abbasi, who served as head of the king's royal library and also inscribed the two major mosques on the royal square, (3) Mir 'Imad, another important calligrapher of this time, and (4) Riza-yi 'Abbasi, the most prominent painter during the reign of Shah 'Abbas, whose portraits of individuals in Isfahan provide an illustrated record of the diverse peoples who populated the city.

SADIQI BEG AFSHAR

Sadiqi Beg Afshar was a master painter who became head of the royal library in 1587. This position would have entailed supervising a large number of individuals associated with specific jobs in manuscript production, including calligraphers and painters. Also working in the library was a younger painter who would later become known as the celebrated Riza-yi 'Abbasi. Together, the two painters and others worked on a *Shahnama* ("Book of Kings"), Abu'l Qasim Firdawsi's (d. 1020) Persian epic poem par excellence, with mythical, legendary, and historical layers narrating Iran's pre-Islamic past until the Arab invasions. They completed the book in 1595.

Sadiqi was, however, a rather difficult person to work with, and approximately one year after completing the *Shahnama* project, he lost his job as head of the library. A calligrapher known as 'Ali Riza 'Abbasi or 'Ali Riza Tabrizi succeeded Sadiqi Beg in 1598. When 'Ali Riza tried to block Sadiqi Beg's career from advancing once he took over as head of the library, Sadiqi Beg complained to Shah 'Abbas that 'Ali Riza was not doing his job. Sadiqi had no success, however, in unseating or discrediting 'Ali Riza, a tough individual who remained in his powerful position and managed to keep all of his opponents at bay.

'ALI RIZA 'ABBASI

'Ali Riza 'Abbasi was born in Tabriz. In 1593, after the Ottomans' campaigns in Azerbaijan (1585–1590), he went to Qazvin, where he underwent training in making inscriptions, inscribing the Friday mosque as part of a refurbishment project that the mosque was undergoing at the time. According to Qazi Ahmad, author of a treatise on calligraphers and painters, the inscriptions in that edifice are "entirely in his luminous writing" (Qazi Ahmad, *Gulistan*, *40*/*Calligraphers* 82). While working on this project, 'Ali Riza 'Abbasi was called to duty by Farhad Khan Qaramanlu, the general whom Shah 'Abbas executed after the Khurasan campaign. Starting in around 1590, he spent two years with Farhad Khan, traveling with him to Khurasan and Mazandaran. He then returned to Qazvin in 1593, when he became part of Shah 'Abbas's court. Shah 'Abbas handsomely rewarded 'Ali Riza 'Abbasi for his significant artistic accomplishments.

While his talents in making inscriptions were outstanding, 'Ali Riza 'Abbasi became better known for his abilities in calligraphy than his inscriptions. He was skilled in numerous calligraphic styles of writing, but perhaps his greatest talent was in writing *nastaliq*, a type of script that combined two forms of calligraphy known as *naskh* and *ta'liq*. Perhaps inspired by nature, music, or human features, *nastaliq* is a beautiful and elegant script that became very popular in the Safavid period not just for works of art, but also for diplomatic correspondence, an occupation in which calligraphers also engaged. Not forgetting his talents in inscription making, Shah 'Abbas asked 'Ali Riza 'Abbasi to inscribe the Shaykh Lutf Allah Mosque and the Royal Mosque on the royal square of Isfahan, and charged him with the task of inscribing the dome, minaret, and gold plaques of the Imam Riza shrine in Mashhad. Shah 'Abbas regarded him so highly that he was a constant presence at the royal court and escorted the king on his travels and his campaigns.

MIR 'IMAD

One of 'Ali Riza's biggest rivals was 'Imad al-Hasani (ca. 1554–1615), another calligrapher. 'Imad al-Hasani, also known as "Mir 'Imad," was born in Qazvin to a family of librarians and accountants. Like 'Ali Riza 'Abbasi, Mir 'Imad showed particular skill in the *nastaliq* form of calligraphy. In addition to producing single-page calligraphic pieces often intended for albums, he also copied works of famous Persian poets such as Hafiz and Sa'di. He did not, however, share 'Ali Riza 'Abbasi's success in staying in favor with the king. Mir 'Imad spent time traveling and working in Qazvin until he succeeded 'Ali Riza 'Abbasi in working for Farhad Khan Qaramanlu in his library in Semnan. In 1599, after the execution of Farhad Khan, he sent a letter to Shah 'Abbas asking for employment in the royal library in Isfahan. His request was granted, and from that time onwards he enjoyed a sixteen-year career as one of the most prominent calligraphers at the court, along with ‘Ali Riza ‘Abbasi.

By the end of that sixteen-year period, Mir ‘Imad seems to have had a falling out with Shah ‘Abbas for reasons that are not entirely clear. Modern scholars and his own contemporaries have mentioned a number of his activities that could have caused him problems. These include spending time with Sufi groups that were out of favor with the king, competing with calligrapher ‘Ali Riza ‘Abbasi, and finally, boasting of his superiority over other artists. There appears to have been a “campaign” of sorts in the royal library, which was headed by ‘Ali Riza ‘Abbasi, to discredit Mir ‘Imad in the eyes of the king. As a result of this campaign, Mir ‘Imad became disappointed in Shah ‘Abbas, presumably for his lack of support. On several occasions he sent the monarch unflattering poetry. This did not go over particularly well, and in 1615 Mir ‘Imad was killed on the charges of harboring Sunni sentiment, with Shah ‘Abbas's implicit approval.

RIZA-YI ‘ABBASI

Mir ‘Imad was not the only artist to have experienced problems working in the royal library. The most prominent Safavid painter during Shah ‘Abbas's reign was Aqa Riza, later known as Riza-yi ‘Abbasi. Like the calligrapher ‘Ali Riza ‘Abbasi, he was part of the court library atelier, joining it some time before 1596. After that time, in 1603, he changed his name to Riza-yi ‘Abbasi (“‘Abbas's Riza”), using ‘Abbasi as a title to indicate his connection to Shah ‘Abbas's court.

Riza-yi ‘Abbasi was best known for his single-page portraits of the people of Isfahan. Some of these portraits were of Isfahan's elites, whom he depicted wearing luxurious garments amidst lavish surroundings, reflecting the new money coming into the city. Others, however, were dervishes, clerics, poets, peasants, and many others of the diverse people he encountered in Isfahan, a cosmopolitan city filled with what must have been fascinating and intriguing individuals to paint. Several of Riza-yi 'Abbasi's portraits bear royal seals, indicating that Shah 'Abbas appreciated or commissioned the work.

Despite his outstanding artistic skills, Riza-yi 'Abbasi experienced a somewhat troubled career at the court. The same chroniclers who sang his praises were also scandalized by the fact that he became addicted to watching wrestling matches. Qazi Ahmad states that:

> (Aqa Rida) [Riza-yi 'Abbasi] is (now) in the most honorable service of the felicitous Shah, lord of the necks (of nations), whose service is supported by the celestial vault, Sultan Shah 'Abbas, may God make his reign eternal. But vicissitudes (of fate) have totally altered Aqa Rida's nature. The company of hapless people and libertines is spoiling his disposition. He is addicted to watching wrestling and to acquiring competence and instruction in this profession.
>
> (Qazi Ahmad, *Calligraphers*, 192–193)

Iskandar Beg, like his teacher Qazi Ahmad, recognizes Riza-yi 'Abbasi's penchant for wrestling and criticizes the people with whom he associated:

> In spite of the delicacy of his touch, he was so uncultured that he became constantly engaged in athletic practices and wrestling, and became infatuated with such habits ... In the service of his present Majesty, the shadow of God, he has been the recipient of favors and kindness and consideration, but on account of his evil ways he has not taken warning and consequently he is always poor and in distress.
>
> (Quoted in Canby, *Rebellious*, 20)

The sequence of events that resulted in Riza-yi 'Abbasi's "rebellion" is unclear. We do know that by 1606, he was fully engrossed with his new preoccupations of wrestling and sports, and as he abandoned the court for several years, dervishes and other "non-courtly subjects," sometimes with anxious or worried looks on their faces, replaced the formal signed portraits for which he was known (Canby, *Rebellious*, 77, 84).

Sheila Canby has compared Riza-yi 'Abbasi's change of heart to a modern-day "midlife crisis." Shah 'Abbas had taken 'Ali Riza the calligrapher and Iskandar Beg Munshi the historian with him during his long period of absence from the court from 1603 to 1607, while on the campaign of Azerbaijan and Shirvan. This resulted in Riza-yi 'Abbasi feeling stranded and seeking the company of wrestlers and others living on the margins of society. He may have become a Sufi and joined a Sufi order, and the criticisms of the people he was associating with at that time actually alluded to the Sufis with whom he was keeping company (Canby, *Rebellious*, 77–84).

In 1610, Riza-yi 'Abbasi returned to the court, apparently out of necessity. Despite his earlier "rebellion," he seems to have remained in Shah 'Abbas's good graces. One of his most famous paintings from the 1620s, depicting a youth reading, bears an inscription stating that the order to produce the work came from the "most noble, most pure Highness." This, and the seal on the painting, suggests that Shah 'Abbas himself commissioned the portrait (Canby, *Shah 'Abbas*, 48–52; Canby, *Rebellious*, 151).

THE ARTS IN DIPLOMACY AND GIFT-GIVING

Works of art were used in both diplomacy and gift-giving, all of which intersected in interesting ways in the Safavid era. As discussed in chapter 5 above, the main aims of diplomatic relations between the Safavids and European powers were to secure an alliance against the Ottomans, to encourage trade, and, in the case of certain European embassies, to promote Christianity to the Safavids and Shah 'Abbas. Gift-giving was an integral part of this diplomatic process in which Shah 'Abbas and various foreign rulers sent embassies back and forth. Many if not most of the objects that changed hands were artistic pieces. This practice served to familiarize the Safavids with Europe and vice versa, and it also allowed for close exchanges with neighbors such as the Mughals.

THE EMBASSY OF KHAN 'ALAM

The practice of gift-giving was part and parcel of the diplomatic etiquette of the time. Kings and other high-ranking officials all participated in it. Shah 'Abbas gave gifts expecting to receive gifts of equal or greater value in return. Artwork played an integral role in the custom of gift-giving. At times, artists took part in the actual diplomatic missions and even depicted the embassies in which the gift-giving took place in their paintings. Perhaps the most frequently illustrated mission was an embassy sent to Shah 'Abbas by the Mughal emperor Jahangir. A brief background of this episode is as follows: Jahangir had come to power in 1605, succeeding his father, the emperor Akbar. In 1613, Jahangir dispatched the ambassador Mirza Barkhurdar, better known as Khan 'Alam, to Iran. This was the first embassy that Jahangir sent to Shah 'Abbas, and he clearly wanted to make it a spectacular event.

Khan Alam also brought numerous impressive gifts for the king, and presented Shah 'Abbas with some "three hundred items, including items of jewelry, bizarre objects, precious stuffs, and so on, and paraded them before the Shah in the Meydan-e Sa'adatabad" (*TAA*, 940/1160).

Khan 'Alam spent approximately five years in Safavid territory, and a great deal of time with the shah, who enjoyed his company. During those years, they met frequently, forging a close relationship that included participating in hunting expeditions, joking, and composing verses. When Khan 'Alam left Iran, he took with him a number of gifts for Jahangir. The most valued items were some 240 paintings of Timur, his descendant, and nobles who fought with Timur against Iletmish Khan.

The embassy made its mark not only on the king, but also on Safavid and Mughal writers and painters, who took great interest in this event. Bishn Das, who accompanied Khan 'Alam to Iran, made a highly influential painting of Shah 'Abbas and Khan 'Alam together. Jahangir wrote about this painting in his memoirs, where he refers to Shah 'Abbas as "my brother." In the Mughal emperor's own words, the painter accompanied the ambassador in order to:

> take the likeness of the shah and his chief statesmen. He had drawn most of them and presented them for my inspection. He had drawn my brother the shah [Shah 'Abbas] in particular very very well. Every one of the shah's servants to whom I showed it said that he had drawn him very well.
>
> (Jahangir, *Jahangirnama*, 319)

In terms of diplomacy, the painting allowed Jahangir to have a sense of what Shah 'Abbas looked like and to gain a better understanding of him by matching a picture to a name. The scene was repainted several times into the late nineteenth century, showing how a historical event captured the popular imagination of later generations.

THE PIERPONT MORGAN PICTURE BIBLE

In addition to being painted by visiting artists, Shah 'Abbas also accepted numerous works of art as gifts from foreign embassies. One of the most interesting gifts that he received was a Bible known today as the "Pierpont Morgan Picture Bible." The Bible dates back to the reign of the French king Louis IX (1226–1270). The ninety-two-page manuscript contains illustrated stories of 340 episodes from the Hebrew Bible, with very little accompanying text. It had made its way to Italy in the late thirteenth century and was in Poland by the early seventeenth century. In 1604, Pope Clement VIII sent an embassy of three Discalced Carmelites to Iran: Father Paul Simon of Jesus Mary, the group leader, Father John Thaddeus of San Eliseus, and Father Vincent of Saint Francis. (Father Vincent's second visit to Iran and audience with Shah 'Abbas, in which he discussed various religious matters with the king, was discussed in chapter 4.) The Carmelites stopped in Poland along the way. Their host, Cardinal Bernard Maciejowski, wanted them to present the Bible to Shah

'Abbas. Cardinal Maciejowski was hoping that with the Bible and other gifts, Shah 'Abbas would look favorably upon Christianity and perhaps be inclined to embrace it himself. He may have even been harboring the hope that the king would send him a gift back.

It took the Carmelites three years after leaving Poland to reach Iran. By the time they finally arrived, Clement VIII and his successor Leo XI, who was in office for merely twenty-five days, had both died and Paul V had become the new pope. As the embassy made its way to Isfahan, the Carmelites were granted an audience with Shah 'Abbas on 3 January 1608. After the king greeted them, they discussed various matters, and presented him with the gifts, one of which was the illustrated Bible. Also included were a "small barrel" of highly regarded Muscovite vodka, for which Shah 'Abbas thanked them profusely, a cross made out of Bohemian glass and decorated with emeralds and other precious stones and a gold Christ, a crystal vase, two paintings, a copy of Euclid in Arabic, and the Gospels (Simpson, "Morgan," 143; *Carmelites* I, 124).

Father Simon wrote a possibly apocryphal account of Shah 'Abbas's reaction upon opening a page of the Bible and chancing on an illustration of the first day of creation:

> When he saw the hideous dragon, vanquished and humiliated at the feet of St. Michael, who brandished his sword threatening the demon, the king inquired: "Who is this who is defeated at the feet of this angel?" Fr. Paul replied, "This is the fallen angel, whom we call the devil." "No," said the shah, laughing greatly, "this is the Turk."
> (Simpson, "Shah 'Abbas," 131–132, 140)

After examining the Bible with great interest, Shah 'Abbas "ordered his majordomo to have one of the wisest mullas study the manuscript and write in Persian language on every illuminated page what is there and what the miniatures mean" (Simpson, "Morgan," 145–146). Marianna Shreve Simpson has suggested that the various additions to the manuscript, such as the Persian captions, Arabic page numbers, and different seals, were made in the royal library. She further states that since the royal library was housed within the palace walls, Shah ʻAbbas could have viewed the manuscript as the annotations and other notations were being added to it (Simpson, "Shah ʻAbbas," 132). There was a precedent to what Shah ʻAbbas did with the Bible gift. In 1602, when a Portuguese mission arrived in Iran by way of Goa, India, they presented Shah ʻAbbas with a copy of the life of Jesus Christ. This book contained small pictures and already had Persian text in the margins. He liked the volume a great deal, and this may have inspired him to have translations placed in the picture Bible that the Carmelites gave him.

Christian kings and clerics were not the only ones who gave Christian-themed gifts. In one instance, when it came time to reciprocate a gift, Shah ʻAbbas sent pictures of figures from the Hebrew Bible done in gold. At various times, he sent to the doge of Venice a piece of cloth made of gold and velvet with a picture of the Annunciation and a piece of velvet with images of Mary, intending both of these items to be used in the San Marco Basilica. He also sent a crucifix that he may have received earlier from Europe, which suggests that re-gifting is not an entirely present-day phenomenon.

Safavid and European artists also influenced each other during this period. The painter Sadiqi Beg made an illustration of the annunciation, drawing inspiration from an engraving made by the "Master of the Banderoles," an anonymous Dutch engraver. Later Safavid paintings continued to show European influence. In 1625, Shah ʻAbbas sent his envoy Musa Beg to Holland, and in the entourage was an artist, Jan Lucasz van Hasselt, who had been living in Isfahan for some time. This embassy did much to generate interest in Iran among Dutch artists. After that embassy, Dutch paintings reflected a marked Persian influence.

INTERNAL GIFT-GIVING

In addition to participation in gift-giving with foreign embassies and visitors to his empire, Shah ʻAbbas presented gifts of art within his own kingdom. Recent scholarship by Kishwar Rizvi has demonstrated how Shah 'Abbas used books and porcelains to promote his public image (Canby, *Shah 'Abbas*, 98–115). For example, in 1607, at approximately the same time that he received the picture Bible, he made a large donation of illustrated books and other items to two shrines: the Safavid family shrine in Ardabil and the shrine of Imam Riza in the city of Mashhad.

The city of Ardabil continued to play a significant role for the Safavid family during the reign of Shah 'Abbas. As the burial place of Shaykh Safi, founder of the Safaviyya Sufi order, Ardabil served as the dynasty's spiritual center. Shah 'Abbas chose to donate to the Ardabil shrine a collection of books on poetry and history, and also a magnificent group of porcelains. So extensive was this collection that he renovated and repurposed a section of the shrine known as the Gunbad-i shahzadaha, renaming it the House of China (*chinikhana*). The renovations included painting, the addition of Qur'anic and Hadith inscriptions on the subjects of victory and the Twelve Imams, and various other improvements. The most significant aspect of the renovation, however, was a modification to allow display of the royal Chinese porcelain collection. This was done by carving plaster niches into the walls of the large room, such that the walls were completely covered with a sort of built-in china cabinet. The niches were custom-fitted to accommodate specific pieces of china, whether a long-necked vase or a ewer or a round jug. Each piece fitted snugly into its own niche. The Safavid kings held these porcelains in very high regard, which explains Shah 'Abbas's desire to display them prominently. In the same room as the porcelain, below the carved niches housing the Chinese porcelains, the books that Shah 'Abbas donated were stored flat on lower shelves, so another function of the room was the provision of space for reading.

We know the extent of Shah 'Abbas's contribution to the shrine because the endowment deed listing the specific items he donated has survived, and at least two of his chroniclers have also listed the gifts. According to Shah 'Abbas's astrologer Munajjim Yazdi, the objects totaled 1162 items, including "Chinese porcelain, Yemeni carnelian and jade cups" (Canby, *Shah 'Abbas*, 121). Iskandar Beg has described the Chinese porcelains as "including large dishes, celadon ware, wine cups, and other Ghurid [modified spelling] and Chinese bowls which were in the royal china store" (*TAA*, 762/955). Some 805 of the porcelains have survived and a number of these have been specifically identified from their descriptions in the sources.

Why would Shah 'Abbas make this kind of donation to the Ardabil shrine when it did not provide any income that would provide salaries or allow further improvements to the shrine? Rizvi has suggested that the move reflects Shah 'Abbas's skills in public relations. The display of porcelains with the carved niches approximates a similar display in the fifth floor of the 'Ali Qapu in Isfahan. However, while only a few select guests could gain entry to the 'Ali Qapu, the general public could view the objects in Ardabil, and in so doing, indirectly experience something of Shah 'Abbas's Persian princely attributes, his public piety, and his wealth and power (Canby, *Shah 'Abbas*, 102–104).

In addition to the donations of porcelains and books to Ardabil, Shah 'Abbas endowed Arabic books on the Qur'an, Islamic jurisprudence, and science to the shrine of Imam Reza in Mashhad. The cleric Shaykh Baha'i, discussed above in chapter 4, played a significant role in choosing which books to donate to Mashhad. The highlight of the library donation was copies of Qur'ans said to contain the signatures of the first three Imams: 'Ali, Hasan, and Husayn. Canby suggests that this donation had a political purpose in that it "would have reflected well on the seriousness of his religious policies" (Canby, *Shah 'Abbas*, 194). Shah 'Abbas also renovated the shrine after the Uzbeks damaged it with their occupation of the city. He donated new doors encrusted with jewels to serve as the entry way into the actual tomb of the Imam, and had the calligrapher 'Ali Riza 'Abbasi write an inscription commemorating Shah 'Abbas's 1601–1602 visit there when the king had the gold dome of the tomb re-gilded.

Shah 'Abbas used the arts to promote his kingship, and this had ramifications in areas such as politics and diplomacy. In befriending and patronizing artists, calligraphers, and painters, and bringing them to Isfahan, he created a style that was recognizable, whether one gazed at miniature paintings or carpets. Shah 'Abbas also engaged in the practice of gift-giving, both internally within his kingdom and externally, as part of his diplomatic activities.

7

THE FINAL PHASE: 1612–1629

The last phase of Shah 'Abbas's rule began with the establishment of two new "capitals" in the Caspian Sea region in 1612 and ended with his death in early 1629. During this period, he continued to orchestrate military campaigns and conquests against the Georgians, Portuguese, Ottomans, and Mughals, he established a royal export monopoly on silk, he dealt with his succession, and he oversaw the further transfer of populations within the empire. In this chapter, we will discuss these issues, the main focal points in the final phase of his life and career.

ASHRAF AND FARAHABAD

Shah 'Abbas spent most of the last seventeen years of his life in two places that we may regard as "new capitals" of the Safavid empire: Farahabad and Ashraf (known today as Beshahr), both in the Caspian Sea province of Mazandaran, his mother's ancestral home. Both cities must have been very attractive to the king, and perhaps because of his preference for hunting and relaxation above devoting all of his time to affairs of state, he did not go to Isfahan at all during the last four years of his life.

Of the two cities, Farahabad was perhaps the more important. Della Valle states that Shah 'Abbas built it for a number of reasons: he wanted to "embellish his kingdom," that is, to ensure that he had developed regions throughout Iran; it was the place from which his mother came; it had the best natural defenses because it was protected by the sea and "wild and barren" mountains; and it was the region farthest from his enemies, especially the Ottomans (Melville, "Itineraries," 214; Della Valle, 176–177/50–51). Farahabad was situated closer to the Caspian Sea. In 1621, he ensured its easy accessibility by widening the roads leading to it. As for Ashraf, it was a planned city like Isfahan, and Shah 'Abbas had a major role in its design. He built a palace there in 1612. According to Iskandar Beg, it had "all necessary ancillary buildings such as bathhouses, workshops, and houses." The chronicler notes that the king "laid out gardens and parks in which nestled attractive residences, each equipped with cisterns" (*TAA*, 855–856/1065–1066). These cisterns contained fountains that sprayed in the likeness of different forms such as flames and fireworks. At the time of Iskandar Beg's writing, in 1629, Ashraf had become, in his words, "a large city and, as a result of the Shah's patronage, a celebrated one" (*TAA*, 856/1066).

Shah 'Abbas used Ashraf and Farahabad as launching points for conquests during the last phase of his life. While the number and duration of his military conquests was less than in previous years, he did lead expeditions into Georgia (1613), Hormuz (1622), Qandahar (1622), and Baghdad (1623).

CAMPAIGNS TO GEORGIA

Shah 'Abbas led campaigns to Georgia at various times in his career as part of his overall aim to bring at least the eastern portion of Georgia under his power and keep it there. Earlier in the Safavid era, although Georgia was caught in the middle of struggles between the Ottomans and the Safavids, the 1555 Treaty of Amasya lent a certain amount of stability to the situation, as the kingdoms into which Georgia was divided came under separate spheres of Ottoman control in the west and Safavid control in the east. In 1590, however, the Peace of Istanbul treaty forced the Safavids to relinquish all of Georgia to the Ottomans.

Shah 'Abbas was quite keen to restore Safavid control over Georgia, but this did not happen until the final phase of his rule. In 1602, he had made the rulers of the two eastern kingdoms previously under Safavid control, Kartli and Kakheti, assist him against the Ottomans. Georgian nobles, however, resisted his influence and placed their own ruler of choice, Teimuraz, on the throne of Kakheti. Shah 'Abbas recognized Teimuraz and he also acknowledged Luarsab II as ruler of Kartli. Despite the king's approval of these individuals, Iskandar Beg Munshi tells us that in 1613, Teimuraz and Luarsab refused Shah 'Abbas's request to meet him in Mazandaran for a hunting expedition, and furthermore, they conspired together against him. As a result, in 1614 Shah 'Abbas went on a campaign to Kartli and Kakheti. Teimuraz and Luarsab II did not surrender but instead fled west to Imereti. In 1615, the nobles of Kakheti rebelled. These actions made Shah 'Abbas even angrier, and his army attacked. Iskandar Beg Munshi states that Kakheti never recovered from the assault, in which the Safavids killed as many as 70,000 people and deported some 100,000 to Iran. Shah 'Abbas then installed 'Isa Khan, Teimuraz's nephew and a convert to Islam, on the throne of Kakheti. As for Luarsab II of Kartli, he surrendered and was sent to Iran, where he was executed in 1622 after he refused to renounce Christianity.

One of the results of the Georgian campaign was Shah 'Abbas's transfer of non-Georgian peoples out of the Kakheti region. These populations of Muslims, Jews, and Armenians had made their way to Kakheti during the Ottoman occupation of Shirvan and Qarabagh. Shah 'Abbas commanded that all non-natives be sent to Mazandaran. He also sent to Farahabad any inhabitants of Shirvan and Qarabagh who had worked under the Ottomans. In this way, some 15,000 families moved to Farahabad and increased the population of the city.

THE ROYAL EXPORT SILK MONOPOLY

Having established rule over Georgia, Shah 'Abbas continued to oversee the economic affairs of his kingdom. After a concerted diplomatic effort to establish new markets for the surplus silk that was being produced in Iran, with the help of the Julfans, Shah 'Abbas established a royal export monopoly on the silk trade. The events that led up to Shah 'Abbas's proclamation of a monopoly on the export of silk were complex, and involved not only the Armenians, but also various outside powers, including first Russia, then the East India Company (EIC) and the Dutch Vereenigde Oostindische Compagnie (VOC), all of whom wanted to export silk from Iran. The EIC, which had interests in selling their cloth to Iran and in exporting silk, reached Iran's interior before the Dutch. They wanted Shah 'Abbas to agree to divert the silk trade away from the overland routes through Anatolia and Ottoman territory and instead travel via the maritime route, as described in chapter 5.

This interest led to competition between the EIC and the Julfan Armenians, who wanted to ensure that they could hold on to their position as the main exporters of Iranian silk through their already established overland routes. In 1619, Shah 'Abbas took advantage of this rivalry to institute a monopoly on the sale of silk. Under this scheme, silk producers had to sell their silk exclusively and at a low cost to Shah 'Abbas, who in turn required anyone wanting to sell it for export to purchase it from him at a fixed rate. In order to establish that fixed rate, he held an auction on 17 September 1619, to "sell" the fixed price to the highest bidder. Three main parties entered the auction: the English, the Julfans, and the Carmelites. In the end, the Julfans won the concession by bidding the highest per-load amount of fifty tumans. The English, who refused to pay the high price that the Julfans were offering, had no silk to sell that year. Overall, the institution of the monopoly, like Shah 'Abbas's other economic reforms, brought further revenue to the crown.

VICTORY IN HORMUZ

The silk trade – and more specifically, the English silk trade – was connected to Shah 'Abbas's victory against the Portuguese in

Hormuz. In 1615, some four years before Shah 'Abbas established the silk monopoly, the EIC had shown interest in selling English broadcloth to Iran. After they approached the shah, he issued an edict (*farman*) allowing them to sell the cloth and to set up a factory, which they did in Jask, an Iranian port city in the Gulf of Oman. A second edict from the king gave the EIC even more wide-ranging privileges, including free trading rights, religious freedom, and a permanent ambassador in Iran. Such privileges were not free for the EIC. The presence of the EIC and the Dutch VOC marks a new phase in European commercial involvement in the Gulf. Shah 'Abbas characteristically played off the rival companies against each other and used them to his advantage, as seen in his use of the English to assist him in expelling the Portuguese from Hormuz.

Since 1515, during the reign of Shah Isma'il, the straits of the Hormuz region had been under Portuguese domination. The Portuguese built a fort on Hormuz island and later added other Persian Gulf ports to their vast seaborne empire. Under Portuguese control, Hormuz flourished as an important commercial center. After Shah 'Abbas came to power, the Safavids could begin to remove the Portuguese from the region. In 1602, with Allahverdi Khan in command, the Safavids had driven the Portuguese out of Bahrain, and in 1614, they took the port city of Gamru (also known as Jarun, Gombroon, and Gombron), which came to be known as Bandar 'Abbas, named after the Shah.

By 1621, Shah 'Abbas was ready to attack Hormuz itself. He was already unhappy with the Portuguese in the aftermath of Don Garcia de Silva y Figueroa's disastrous embassy to Iran. Philip III had sent Don Garcia to Iran after Shah 'Abbas requested that "some gentleman of note" visit him. Don Garcia arrived in Isfahan in 1617, but his message consisted of a demand that the Safavids return the island of Qishm, the Bahrain islands, and other areas to the Portuguese. In 1620, the Portuguese fought and lost two naval battles against the English for control over the Gulf. In 1621, taking advantage of the commercial and diplomatic privileges he had extended to the EIC, Shah 'Abbas demanded that they assist him in removing the Portuguese from Hormuz, or else he would remove their trading privileges. The English agreed to assist the shah, and the campaign began.

Shah 'Abbas did not personally lead this operation; instead, he appointed Imamquli Khan, Allahverdi Khan's son, to be in charge. Using Gombron as his base, Imamquli Khan began by attacking the fort in Hormuz with the assistance of English ships that transported his troops to the island. After a brutal two-month siege, in the spring of 1622, Imamquli Khan destroyed the fortress and defeated the Portuguese, who sought terms of surrender and were handed over to the English, according to a previous agreement made between the English and the Safavids. At the same time, the island of Qishm also fell to the Safavids. Shah 'Abbas appointed officers to administer Hormuz and ensure that it would not be used for commercial purposes against Iran. This in turn led to Bandar 'Abbas becoming an important Safavid port.

The Dutch VOC, aware of the Safavid victory at Hormuz, sent their representative Hubert Visnich to establish a treaty with the shah, which he did in 1623. This treaty gave the VOC a specific amount of silk at a fixed rate and the VOC were allowed to export into Iran a specified amount of goods without having to pay any tolls. However, the VOC and the EIC were required to pay in the local currency for a portion of the goods they purchased, because Shah 'Abbas needed the income.

THE TAKING OF QANDAHAR

Having taken care of the Portuguese, Shah 'Abbas could look eastward one last time and attempt to recapture Qandahar from the Mughals. We left Qandahar when the Mughals seized it from Shah 'Abbas in 1595. At that time, the monarch was too weak to hold on to the city. His approach in the decades until he finally could attempt retaking it says a great deal about his ability to think strategically, and to do so on a long-term basis while in a position of relative weakness. His main tactic appears to have been one of befriending the new Mughal emperor Jahangir, son of the celebrated Mughal king Akbar, who died in 1605, and corresponding with him even before he became emperor. Shah ʻAbbas had made one attempt in 1604 to take the fortress in Qandahar, but it failed, and he later claimed that he knew nothing about the scheme, as governors from Farah and Sistan, assisted by Qizilbash troops from Herat, had carried out the campaign that the governor of Herat had allegedly orchestrated. This, however, was merely a face-saving statement after the fact, for one of his chroniclers indicates that he was in constant communication with the commanders carrying out the operation.

Subsequently, Shah ʻAbbas repeatedly sent envoys and emissaries to the Mughal court in order to cultivate good relations between himself and Jahangir, and perhaps to broach the subject of the Mughals "returning" Qandahar to the Safavids. These embassies did not yield any substantial results, and with the exception of Khan ʻAlam's embassy to the Safavid court in 1613, discussed in chapter 6, all of the diplomatic traffic flowed from the Safavids to the Mughals. In 1620, after Khan ʻAlam's showy embassy, Shah ʻAbbas sent an equally impressive return mission to Jahangir, headed by Zaynal Beg. In addition to the usual striking collection of gifts, Zaynal Beg was tasked with negotiating the Mughals' handing over of Qandahar to the Safavids, but unsurprisingly had no success in accomplishing this. Shah ʻAbbas subsequently sent several more embassies to the Mughals, always carrying gifts and offering friendship.

These embassies were not entirely without result, for Shah ʻAbbas used information he obtained about intrigue at Jahangir's court to launch his attack against the Mughals. He headed out from Isfahan in February 1622. At this time, Jahangir's wife Nur Jahan Begum, with whom he had no children, had had a falling out with her step-son, Prince Shah Jahan. When Jahangir learned of Shah ʻAbbas's advance, he was surprised, due to the friendly gestures that Shah 'Abbas had made over the years. He candidly expresses this surprise in his memoirs: "Several days prior to this, reports had been received from officials in Kandahar telling of the ruler of Iran's campaign against Kandahar. In view of our past and present relations, I couldn't believe it" (Jahangir, *Jahangirnama*, 378). Jahangir ordered his son Shah Jahan to go to Qandahar, but he refused, fearing that his step-mother Nur Jahan Begum would use his absence to her advantage. Nur Jahan, on her part, still used the opportunity to denounce Shah Jahan, only this time she accused him of being a rebel for not obeying his father. The Mughal fortress in Qandahar fell to the Safavids after a five- to six-week siege. Shah Jahan did, in fact, launch an actual rebellion against his father that lasted some four years, and diverted Shah Jahan's attention away from any attempt to retake Qandahar.

THE TAKING OF BAGHDAD

The last major military victory that Shah 'Abbas experienced before his death was the retaking of Baghdad, which had been under Ottoman control since the Ottomans took the city from Shah Tahmasb in 1534. The entire region loomed very large in Safavid consciousness, particularly Baghdad and the area known as the 'Atabat, a pilgrimage destination consisting of the holy cities of Najaf, where the Imam 'Ali is buried; Karbala, home to the shrine of Imam Husayn; Kazemayn, where Imam Musa al-Kazim – the Seventh Imam from whom the Safavids claimed physical descent – and Muhammad al-Taqi, the Ninth Imam, are buried; and finally Samarra, where the shrines of 'Ali al-Naqi and Hasan al-'Askari, the Tenth and Eleventh Imams, are located. Due to the religious and ideological importance of the area, the Safavids consistently claimed central Mesopotamia (central Iraq), despite the fact that they did not actually control Baghdad and central Mesopotamia for very long. The Safavids were in power for 220 years and held central Iraq for a mere forty-two of those years, the area being separated from Iran by the Zagros mountains.

Shah 'Abbas made his move after the assassination of the Ottoman Sultan Osman II on 20 May 1620. The ensuing chaos and weakness of the Ottoman empire, in addition to widespread rebellion, created ideal conditions for him to attack. His campaign into Iraq started when the governor of Baghdad, in rebellion against the Ottoman crown, asked him for assistance. Shah 'Abbas succeeded in taking Baghdad, but did not manage to capture Basra. The Safavid chronicles, in justifying the campaign, suggest that Shah 'Abbas found inspiration for the military expedition after he went on a long-desired pilgrimage to the 'Atabat, but the Ottoman sources say nothing of the sort, emphasizing instead the devastation that the Safavids brought to Baghdad.

SUCCESSION TO THE THRONE

During this last phase of Shah 'Abbas's life, in addition to the transfer of populations and the military conquests described here, he had his two remaining sons blinded. Shah 'Abbas had a total of five sons. He had his first son, Muhammad Baqir (also known as Safi), executed in 1615 amidst fears that he was becoming too powerful and popular, and conspiring against his father. His second son Hasan and his fourth son Isma'il died as children. This left him with two sons who could have succeeded to the throne, and these were the two whom he had blinded: his third son Muhammad Mirza (Muhammad Khudabanda) in 1621 and his fifth son Imam Quli Mirza in 1627. In this way, Shah 'Abbas ensured their inability to rule after his death.

Why would a king blind his sons? At least one scholar has suggested that Shah 'Abbas's early life caused him to be somewhat paranoid about his own sons conspiring against him. Beyond this specific context, evidence points to Shah 'Abbas's more general fears about attempts on his own life. The traveler Pietro Della Valle suggests that some of the king's seemingly eccentric behavior reflects this concern:

> Owing to an apprehension of attempts of this kind [i.e. poisoning], it is, in my opinion, that the King does so many things which ignorant people tax as whimsical and unworthy of Majesty; such for example as cooking for himself, which is common with him, particularly the fish or game he has himself caught or killed ... At other times he will dine in the streets from cooks' shops wherever any grateful odour salutes him from the steaming kitchens. In this he is not particular, many individuals, on account of the superior cooking at these shops, being served from them with their meals. Again, in riding along His Majesty will enter a house, and dine on whatever the family may have provided for itself.
>
> (Della Valle, 82–83/33)

SHAH 'ABBAS'S DEATH

Late in 1628, Shah 'Abbas was in Qazvin receiving the governor of Qandahar. At that time, he was in the midst of suffering repeated bouts of quartan fever, a form of malaria. Inappropriate amounts of activity caused him to relapse. Despite warnings from his doctors about the unsuitably wet climate in the Caspian region, the king very much wanted to spend the winter in Mazandaran, and ultimately decided to make the journey there from Qazvin, planning a slower pace that would make the trip last twenty-four days – double the amount of time it would normally take him to get there. Despite these intentions, his enthusiasm and desire to reach his destination got the better of him, and he ended up reaching Ashraf in just nine days – some three days fewer than the normal travel time. By the time he arrived in Ashraf, his fever had returned, yet he still proceeded to engage in hunting and tend to state affairs. After one such hunting expedition, he returned home quite ill, and was confined to bed, becoming increasingly weak until he died on 19 January 1629.

SUCCESSION AND FUNERAL

Shortly before his death, Shah 'Abbas had nominated his grandson Sam Mirza, son of Muhammad Baqir (Safi), as his successor. Once notice was sent to Isfahan of the king's death, Sam Mirza was quickly seated on the throne there as Shah Safi, and arrangements were made for Shah 'Abbas's funeral.

Shah 'Abbas's funeral procession included his aunt and other women of the harem. The procession went from Mazandaran to Kashan, where multitudes of people came to pay their respects. His body was kept in state at the shrine of Imamzada Habib, son of the Seventh Imam Musa al-Kazim, in Kashan. Iskandar Beg describes the scene at the shrine, where the large crowds made it difficult for notables to pay their respect (*TAA*, 1078–1079/1303–1304). Teams of individuals who had memorized the Qur'an recited it continuously, and they burned candles all night. Food was provided to the Qur'an reciters, the poor, and the shrine keepers, and this continued until a Qizilbash from the Qajar tribe, a certain Mahdi Qoli Beg, supervised the king's burial.

CONCLUSIONS

Shah 'Abbas was sixty years old when he died, and thus ended a remarkable forty-two-year reign on the Safavid throne. His rule made a tremendous impact, and his policies and actions altered the political, religious, social, and cultural landscapes of Safavid Iran. From the start, he was quick to seize every opportunity he could to shape events to his benefit. He swiftly consolidated his rule upon coming to power, eliminating both internal and external threats. While he flirted with religious heterodox movements early in his reign, he soon distanced himself from such movements and started to align his state with orthodox expressions of Shi'i Islam.

Upon moving the Safavid capital to Isfahan, Shah 'Abbas established centralized rule in a number of ways, most notably by instituting a broad series of economic reforms and reshaping Safavid society in a way that made all the constituent elements remain loyal to him. The majestic buildings that rest on the great square are but one reflection of the power he projected in his new capital. The bazaars in Isfahan were full of goods, reflecting his openness to trade and commerce, as the city became a cosmopolitan center. The roads by which those goods were delivered to the bazaars were kept safe, and merchants could rest at any number of new caravanserais that he built. Close by in the suburb of New Julfa lived the Armenian community, which he forcibly moved to Isfahan, but which came to constitute a new elite in Isfahan, along with the *ghulam*s who formed Shah 'Abbas's new army and became important officials. With land revenues coming into his treasury as a result of his transformation of provincial land into crown land, Shah 'Abbas could afford to pay for his new city, his new army, and the administrators who helped run the Safavid state.

Shah 'Abbas enhanced his economic reform program by using religion to his political advantage. He combined public acts of piety, such as traveling to Mashhad on foot, which had an added economic and political benefit, with public acts of traditional kingly behavior, such as drinking and enjoying popular entertainment, to show that he was both devout and at the same time above religious laws. In encouraging religious thinkers to explore new ideas, Shi'i Islam acquired a depth that could stand up to religious developments taking place in Ottoman Sunnism. He also welcomed Christian missionaries into Iran, some of whom harbored hopes that he would convert, and used their presence to further his political ambitions. He similarly received ambassadors into Iran and sent his own emissaries both east and west. While the plans to form an anti-Ottoman alliance or to divert the silk trade that the messages relayed did not materialize, Shah 'Abbas took advantage of the European presence in his kingdom to engage in more successful military campaigns and to promote the silk trade.

Shah 'Abbas used his position as king to promote the arts, and the arts, in turn, promoted the king. As accomplished artists flocked to Isfahan, they helped create an imperial brand that helped boost Shah 'Abbas's public image. Carpets, woven from the silk that was being produced in the country, bound books, illustrated by artists that the king promoted, and other works of art contained familiar features that were recognizable and came to be associated with his era. Such impressive pieces often became gifts that Shah 'Abbas used in embassies and exchanges.

As the state became stable, Shah 'Abbas spent the last phase of his life in the Caspian Sea region. While he did not exactly go into retirement, he obviously felt that his direct presence was not needed in Isfahan. Still, during this final phase, he ousted the Portuguese from Hormuz, captured Qandahar from the Mughals and Baghdad from the Ottomans, and established the royal export monopoly on silk.

Overall, perhaps his greatest success was in incorporating into the state the "new constituencies" such as the *ghulam*s, the Armenians, and the Shi'i clerics, without completely marginalizing older constituencies (Newman, *Safavid*, 71). While some scholarly assessments of Shah 'Abbas suggest that Iran went into a period of "decline" after he died, the Safavid dynasty nevertheless remained in power for nearly a century following his death.

FURTHER READING

The following works were consulted in several chapters of this book and/ or are suggested for further reading:

SECONDARY WORKS

Abisaab, Rula Jurdi. *Converting Persia: Religion and Power in the Safavid Empire*. London: I. B. Tauris, 2004.

Arjomand, Said Amir. *The Shadow of God and the Hidden Imam: Religion, Political Order, and Societal Change in Shi'ite Iran from the Beginning to 1890*. Chicago: University of Chicago Press, 1984.

Babaie, Sussan, Kathryn Babayan, Ina Baghdiantz-McCabe, and Massumeh Farhad. *Slaves of the Shah: New Elites of Safavid Persia*. London: I. B. Tauris, 2004.

Babayan, Kathryn. *Mystics, Monarchs, and Messiahs: Cultural Landscapes of Early Modern Iran*. Cambridge, MA: Harvard University Center for Middle Eastern Studies, 2002.

Blow, David. *Shah 'Abbas: the Ruthless King Who Became an Iranian Legend*. London: I. B. Tauris, 2009.

Canby, Sheila R. *Shah 'Abbas: the Remaking of Isfahan*. London: British Museum Press, 2009.

Encyclopædia Iranica. Online edition. www.iranicaonline.org.

Encyclopedia of Islam. Online edition. http://referenceworks.brillonline.com/browse/encyclopaedia-of-islam–2.

Falsafi, Nasr Allah. *Zindagani-yi Shah 'Abbas-i avval*. Tehran: Intisharat-i 'Ilmi, 1966.

Jackson, Peter and Laurence Lockhart, eds. *The Cambridge History of*

Iran. Vol. 6: The Timurid and Safavid Periods. Cambridge: Cambridge University Press, 1986.

Matthee, Rudolph P. *The Politics of Trade in Safavid Iran: Silk for Silver 1600–1730*. Cambridge: Cambridge University Press, 1999.

Newman, Andrew. *Safavid Iran: Rebirth of a Persian Empire*. London: I. B. Tauris, 2006.

Savory, Roger. *Iran under the Safavids*. Cambridge: Cambridge University Press, 1980.

Streusand, Douglas E. *Islamic Gunpowder Empires: Ottomans, Safavids, and Mughals*. Boulder, CO: Westview Press, 2011.

PRIMARY SOURCES

A Chronicle of the Carmelites in Persia and the Papal Mission of the XVIIth and XVIIIth Centuries, ed. H. Chick, 2 vols. London: Eyre & Spottiswoode, 1939.

Della Valle, Pietro. *I Viaggi di Pietro Della Valle*, eds F. Gaeta and L. Lockhart. [Rome]: Istituto Poligrafico dello Stato, Libreria dello Stato, 1972. Trans. [Select Writings]. In *A General Collection of the Best and Most Interesting Voyages and Travels in All Parts of the World*, vol. 9 [Asia], ed. John Pinkerton. London: Longman, Hurst, Rees, and Orme [etc.], 1811.

Don Juan. *Don Juan of Persia: a Shi'ah Catholic 1560–1604*, trans. Guy Le Strange. New York: George Routledge & Sons Ltd., 1926.

Iskandar Beg Munshi. *Tarikh-i 'alamara-yi 'Abbasi*, 2nd ed. 2 vols, ed. Iraj Afshar. Tehran: Amir Kabir, 1350 [1971]; trans. Roger Savory as *History of Shah 'Abbas the Great*, 3 vols. Boulder, CO: Westview Press, 1978.

Qazi Ahmad Munshi Qummi. *Gulistan-i hunar*, ed. Ahmad Suhayli Khvansari. [Tehran]: Intisharat-i Bunyad va Farhang-i Iran, n.d.; trans. V. Minorsky as *Calligraphers and Painters*. Washington: Smithsonian Institution, 1959.

Siyaqi Nizam. "Fotuhat-e homayun: 'Les Victoires augustes,' 1007/1598," ed., trans., and ann., Chahryar Adle. PhD dissertation. Paris, 1976.

BIBLIOGRAPHY

CHAPTER 1

EI2 articles:
"al-Karaki." Madelung, W.

Amini Haravi, Sadr al-Din Sultan Ibrahim. *Futuhat-i shahi*, ed. Muhammad Riza Nasiri. Tehran: Anjuman-i Asar va Mafakhir-i Farhangi, 1383 [2004].

Arjomand, Said Amir. "The Rise of Shah Esma'il as a Mahdist Revolution." *Studies in Persianate Societies* 3 (2005): 44–65.

Babayan, Kathryn. "The Safavid Synthesis: from Qizilbash Islam to Imamite Shi'ism." *Iranian Studies* 27 (1994): 135–161.

Brummett, Palmira. "The Myth of Shah Ismail Safavi: Political Rhetoric and 'Divine' Kingship," in *Medieval Christian Perceptions of Islam*, ed. John Victor Tolan, 326–352. London: Routledge, 2000.

Grey, C., trans. and ed. "The Travels of a Merchant in Persia," in *A Narrative of Italian Travels in Persia, in the Fifteenth and Sixteenth Centuries*. London: Printed for the Hakluyt Society, 1873.

Khunji, Fazl Allah ibn Ruzbihan. *Tarikh-i 'alam'ara-yi Amini*, trans. and abr. V. Minorsky, rev. and aug. John E. Woods. London: Royal Asiatic Society, 1992.

Khvandamir, Ghiyas al-Din. *Tarikh-i habib al-siyar*, 4 vols., ed. Jalal al-Din Huma'i. [Tehran]: Kitabkhanah-'i Khayyam, 1333 [1954]; trans. Wheeler Thackston as *Habibu's-siyar*, 2 vols. Cambridge, MA: Harvard University Department of Near Eastern Languages and Civilizations, 1994.

Membré, Michele. *Mission to the Lord Sophy of Persia (1539–1542)*, trans. A. H. Morton. London: School of Oriental and African Studies, 1993.

Minorsky, Vladimir. "The Poetry of Shah Isma'il I." *Bulletin of the School of Oriental and African Studies* 10 (1942): 1006–1053.

Morton, A. H. "The Chub-i Tariq and Qizilbash Ritual in Safavid Persia," in *Etudes Safavides*, ed. Jean Calmard, 225–245. Paris and Tehran: L'Institut français de Recherche en Iran, 1993.

Savory, Roger M. "The Office of Khalifat al-Khulafa under the Safawids." *Journal of the American Oriental Society* 85 (1965): 497–502.

Shirazi, Abdi Beg. *Takmilat al-akhbar*, ed. 'Abd al-Husayn Nava'i. Tehran: Nashr-i Nay, 1990.

Tavakkul ibn Isma'il, ibn Bazzaz. *Safvat al-safa*, ed. Ghulam Riza Tabataba'i Majd. Ardabil: G. Tabataba'i Majd, 1994.

CHAPTER 2

EI2 articles:

"Nimat Allahiyya." Algar, Hamid.

"Nuktawiyya." Algar, Hamid.

EIR articles:

"Allahverdi Khan (1)." Savory, Roger M.

"Farhad Khan Qaramanlu." Matthee, Rudi.

"Kandahar iv. From the Mongol Invasion Through the Safavid Era." Matthee, Rudi and Hiroyuki Mashita.

Afushtah'i Natanzi, Mahmud ibn Hidayat Allah. *Naqavat al-asar fi zikr al-akhyar*, ed. Ihsan Ishraqi. Tehran: Bungah-i Tarjumah va Nashr-i Kitab, 1971.

Bagashvili, Valerian N. "The Undiladze Feudal House in the Sixteenth to Seventeenth-Century Iran According to the Georgian Sources." *Iranian Studies* 40 (2007): 37–58.

Dale, Stephen F. *The Muslim Empires of the Ottomans, Safavids, and Mughals*. Cambridge: Cambridge University Press, 2010.

Islam, Riazul. *Indo-Persian Relations: a Study of the Political and Diplomatic Relations between the Mughul Empire and Iran*. Tehran: Iranian Culture Foundation, 1970.

Lambton, Ann K. S. "Justice in the Medieval Persian Theory of Kingship." *Studia Islamica* 17 (1962): 91–119.

Lambton, Ann K. S. "Quis custodiet custodes? Some Reflections on the Persian Theory of Government (Conclusion)." *Studia Islamica* 6 (1956): 125–146.

Maeda, Hirotake. "Exploitation of the Frontier: the Caucasus Policy of Shah 'Abbas I," in *Iran and the World in the Safavid Age*, ed. Willem Floor and Edmund Herzig, 471–489. London: I. B. Tauris, 2012.

Maeda, Hirotake. "The Forced Migrations and Reorganisation of the Regional Order in the Caucasus by Safavid Iran: Preconditions and Developments Described by Fazli Khuzani," in *Reconstruction and Interaction of Slavic Eurasia and Its Neighboring Worlds*, ed. Ieda Osamu and Uyama Tomohiko, 237–271. Sapporo: Slavic Research Center, Hokkaido University, 2006.

Matthee, Rudi. "Loyalty, Betrayal, and Retribution: Biktash Khan, Ya'qub Khan, and Shah 'Abbas I's Strategy in Establishing Control over Kirman, Yazd and Fars," in *Ferdowsi, the Mongols, and the History of Iran: Art, Literature and Culture from Early Islam to Qajar Persia*, ed. Robert Hillenbrand, A. C. S. Peacock, and Firuza Abdullaeva, 184–200. London: I. B. Tauris, 2013.

Mirjafari, Hossein. "The Haydari-Ni'mati Conflicts in Iran," trans. J. R. Perry. *Iranian Studies* 12 (1979): 135–162.

Perry, John R. "Toward a Theory of Iranian Urban Moieties: the Haydariyyah and Ni'matiyyah Revisited." *Iranian Studies* 32 (1999): 51–70.

Qazi Ahmad Munshi Qummi. *Khulasat al-tavarikh*, ed. Ihsan Ishraqi, 2 vols. Tehran: Danishgah-i Tihran, 1984.

Quinn, Sholeh. *Historical Writing during the Reign of Shah 'Abbas: Ideology, Imitation, and Legitimacy in Safavid Chronicles*. Salt Lake City: University of Utah Press, 2000.

Rahimlu, Yusof and Jawad Qasemi. "'Abbas I," in *Encyclopaedia Islamica*, ed. Wilferd Madelung and Farhad Daftary. Brill Online, 2013.

Streusand, Douglas E. *The Formation of the Mughal Empire*. Delhi: Oxford University Press, 1989.

CHAPTER 3

EIR articles:

"Ali Qapu." Soucek, P. P.

"Armenia and Iran vi. Armeno-Iranian Relations in the Islamic Period." Bournoutian, G.

"Della Valle, Pietro." Gurney, John.

"Deportations." Perry, John R.
"Isfahan x. Monuments (3) Mosques." Babaie, Sussan with Robert Haug.
"Julfa iv. Architecture and Painting." Haghnazarian, Armen.

Arak'el, Dawrizhets'i. *The History of Vardapet Arak'el of Tabriz, Volume I*, trans. George A. Bournoutian. Costa Mesa, CA: Mazda Publishers, 2005.
Aslanian, Sebouh David. *From the Indian Ocean to the Mediterranean: the Global Trade Networks of Armenian Merchants from New Julfa*. Berkeley: University of California Press, 2011.
Babaie, Sussan. *Isfahan and Its Palaces: Statecraft, Shi'ism and the Architecture of Conviviality in Early Modern Iran*. Edinburgh: Edinburgh University Press, 2008.
Blake, Stephen P. *Half the World: the Social Architecture of Safavid Isfahan, 1590–1722*. Costa Mesa, CA: Mazda Publishers, 1999.
Della Valle, Pietro. [Select Writings]. In *A General Collection of the Best and Most Interesting Voyages and Travels in All Parts of the World*, vol. 9 [Asia], ed. John Pinkerton. London: Longman, Hurst, Rees, and Orme [etc.], 1811.
Durand-Guédy, David. *Iranian Elites and Turkish Rulers: a History of Isfahan in the Saljuq Period*. London: Routledge, 2010.
Herzig, Edmund M. "The Armenian Merchants of New Julfa, Isfahan: a Study in Pre-modern Asian Trade." PhD dissertation. Oxford, 1991.
Herzig, Edmund. "The Deportation of the Armenians in 1604–1605 and Europe's Myth of Shah 'Abbas I," in *Safavid Persia: the History and Politics of an Islamic Society*, ed. Charles Melville, 59–71. London: I. B. Tauris, 1996.
Matthee, Rudi. "Prostitutes, Courtesans, and Dancing Girls: Women Entertainers in Safavid Iran," in *Iran and Beyond: Essays in Middle Eastern History in Honor of Nikki R. Keddie*, ed. Rudi Matthee and Beth Baron, 121–150. Costa Mesa, CA: Mazda Publishers, 2000.
McChesney, Robert D. "Four Sources on Shah 'Abbas's Building of Isfahan." *Muqarnas* 5 (1988): 103–134.

CHAPTER 4

EI2 articles:
"Mulla Sadra Shirazi." MacEoin, D.
"al-Suhrawardi." Ziai, Hossein.

EIR articles:

"Ahmad Alawi." Corbin, H.

"Baha-al-Din 'Ameli." Kohlberg, E.

"Damad, Mir(-e), Sayyed Mohammed Baqer." Newman, Andrew J.

"Emam-e jom'a." Algar, Hamid.

"Karaki." Abisaab, Rula Jurdi.

al-'Amili, Shaykh Baha' al-Din. *Jami'-i 'Abbasi*. S.L., N.P., 1855?

Matthee, Rudolph P. *The Pursuit of Pleasure: Drugs and Stimulants in Iranian History, 1500–1900*. Princeton: Princeton University Press, 2005.

Meisami, Sayeh. *Mulla Sadra*. London: Oneworld, 2013.

Melville, Charles. "From Qars to Qandahar: the Itineraries of Shah 'Abbas I (995–1038/1587–1629)," in *Etudes Safavides*, ed. Jean Calmard, 195–224. Paris and Tehran: L'Institut français de Recherche en Iran, 1993.

Melville, Charles. "Shah 'Abbas and the Pilgrimage to Mashhad," in *Safavid Persia: the History and Politics of an Islamic Society*, ed. Charles Melville, 191–229. London: I. B .Tauris, 1996.

Nasr, Seyyed Hossein. *Sadr al-Din Shirazi and His Transcendent Theosophy: Background, Life and Works*. Tehran: Imperial Iranian Academy of Philosophy, 1978.

CHAPTER 5

EIR articles:

"Amasya, Peace of." Kohbach, M.

"Ango-Iranian Relations i. Safavid to Zand Periods." Ferrier, R. W.

"Barut." Floor, W.

"Della Valle, Pietro." Gurney, John.

"Farhad Khan Qaramanlu, Rokn al-Saltana." Matthee, Rudi.

"Firearms i. History." Matthee, Rudi.

"Firearms ii. Production of Cannon and Muskets." Mohebbi, Parviz.

"Portugal i. Relations with Persia in the Early Modern Age." Teles e Cunha, Joao.

Dickson, Martin B. "Shah Tahmasb and the Uzbeks: the Duel for Khurasan with 'Ubayd Khan (930–946/1524–1540)." PhD dissertation. Princeton, 1958.

Gurney, J. D. "Pietro della Valle: the Limits of Perception." *Bulletin of the School of Oriental and African Studies* 49 (1986): 103–116.

Loureiro, Rui Manuel. "The Persian Ventures of Fr. António de Gouveia." In *Portugal, the Persian Gulf and Safavid Persia*, ed. Rudi Matthee and Jorge Flores, 249–264. Leuven: Peeters, in Association with the Iran Heritage Foundation and the Freer Gallery of Art & Arthur M. Sackler Gallery, Smithsonian Institution, 2011.

Matthee, Rudi. "Anti-Ottoman Politics and Transit Rights: the Seventeenth-Century Trade in Silk between Safavid Iran and Muscovy." *Cahiers du Monde Russe* 35 (1994): 739–761.

Matthee, Rudi. "Unwalled Cities and Restless Nomads: Firearms and Artillery in Safavid Iran," in *Safavid Persia: the History and Politics of an Islamic Society*, ed. Charles Melville, 389–416. London: I. B. Tauris, 1996.

McChesney, Robert D. "The Conquest of Herat 995–6/1587–8: Sources for the Study of Safavid/Qizilbash-Shibanid/Uzbak Relations," in *Etudes Safavides*, ed. Jean Calmard, 69–107. Paris and Tehran: L'Institut français de Recherche en Iran, 1993.

Niayesh, Ladan. "Shakespeare's Persians." *Shakespeare* 4 (2008): 137–147.

Quinn, Sholeh A. "Historical Writing during the Reign of Shah 'Abbas I." PhD dissertation. Chicago, 1993.

Savory, R. M. "The Sherley Myth." *Iran* 5 (1967): 73–81.

Sherley, Anthony. *Sir Anthony Sherley and His Persian Adventure*, ed. Sir E. Denison Ross. London: G. Routledge & Sons, 1933.

Steensgaard, Niels. *The Asian Trade Revolution of the Seventeenth Century*. Chicago: University of Chicago Press, 1973.

Zarinebaf-Shahr, Fariba. "The Iranian Merchant Community in the Ottoman Empire and the Constitutional Revolution," in *Les Iraniens d'Istanbul*, ed. Thierry Zarcone and Fariba Zarinebaf-Shahr, 203–212. Istanbul: Institut français d'études anatoliennes; Louvain, Belgique: Diffusion, Peeters, 1993.

CHAPTER 6

EIR articles:

"'Ali-Reza 'Abbasi." Soucek, P. P.

"Art in Iran ix. Safavid to Qajar Periods." Welch, A.

"Calligraphy." Yusofi, Golam-Hosayn.
"'Emad Hasani, Mir, 'Emad-al-Molk." Eslami, Kambiz.

Canby, Sheila. *The Golden Age of Persian Art 1501–1722*. London: British Museum Press, 2008.

Canby, Sheila R. *The Rebellious Reformer: the Drawings and Paintings of Riza-yi 'Abbasi of Isfahan*. London: Azimuth Editions, 1996.

Goetz, Hermann. "Persian and Persian Costumes in Dutch Painting of the Seventeenth Century." *Art Bulletin* 20 (1938): 280–290.

Grube, Ernst J. and Eleanor Sims. "The Representations of Shah 'Abbas I," in *L'arco di Fango che Rubò la Luce alle Stelle: Studi in Onore di Eugenio Galdieri per Il Suo Settantesimo Compleanno: Roma 29 Ottobre 1995*, ed. M. Bernardini et al., 177–208. Lugano: Edizioni Arte e Moneta, 1995.

Islam, Riazul. *Indo-Persian Relations: a Study of the Political and Diplomatic Relations between the Mughul Empire and Iran*. Tehran, Iranian Culture Foundation, 1970.

Jahangir. *The Jahangirnama: Memoirs of Jahangir, Emperor of India*, trans., ed., and ann. Wheeler M. Thackston. New York: Freer Gallery of Art, Arthur M. Sackler Gallery in Association with Oxford University Press, 1999.

McChesney, Robert D. "Four Sources on Shah 'Abbas's Building of Isfahan." *Muqarnas* 5 (1988): 103–134.

Qazi Ahmad Munshi Qummi. *Gulistan-i hunar*, ed. Ahmad Suhayli Khvansari. [Tehran]: Intisharat-i Bunyad va Farhang-i Iran, n.d.; trans. V. Minorsky as *Calligraphers and Painters*. Washington: Smithsonian Institution, 1959.

Simpson, Marianna Shreve. "Gifts for the Shah: an Episode in Hapsburg–Safavid Relations during the Reigns of Philip III and 'Abbas I," in *Gifts of the Sultan: the Arts of Giving at the Islamic Courts*, ed. Linda Komaroff, 125–139. Los Angeles: Los Angeles County Museum of Art; New Haven: Yale University Press, 2011.

Simpson, Marianna Shreve. "The Morgan Bible and the Giving of Religious Gifts between Iran and Europe/Europe and Iran during the Reign of Shah 'Abbas I," in *Between the Picture and the Word: Manuscript Studies from the Index of Christian Art*, ed. Colum Hourihane, 141–150. Princeton, N.J.: Index of Christian Art, Dept. of Art and Archaeology, Princeton University in Association with Penn State Press, 2005.

Simpson, Marianna Shreve. "Shah 'Abbas and His Picture Bible," in *The Book of Kings: Art, War, and the Morgan Library's Medieval Picture Bible*, ed. William Noell and Daniel Weiss, 121–141. London: Third Millennium Pub.; [Baltimore]: Walters Art Museum.

Soudavar, Abolala. *Art of the Persian Courts: Selections from the Art and History Trust Collection*. New York: Rizzoli, 1992.

CHAPTER 7

EIR articles:

"Atabat." Algar, H.

"Dutch-Persian Relations." Floor, Willem.

"Georgia ii. History of Iranian-Georgian Relations." Hitchens, Keith.

"Hormuz ii. Islamic Period." Floor, Willem.

"Iraq iv. Relations in the Safavid Period." Matthee, Rudi.

Beradze, Grigol. "On the History of the Political Relations of Safavid Iran and Georgia: King Luarsab II and His Captivity in Iran," in *Iran and the World in the Safavid Age*, ed. Willem Floor and Edmund Herzig, 459–470. London: I. B. Tauris, 2012.

Islam, Riazul. *Indo-Persian Relations: a Study of the Political and Diplomatic Relations between the Mughul Empire and Iran*. Tehran: Iranian Culture Foundation, 1970.

Jahangir. *The Jahangirnama: Memoirs of Jahangir, Emperor of India*, trans., ed., and ann. Wheeler M. Thackston. New York: Freer Gallery of Art, Arthur M. Sackler Gallery in Association with Oxford University Press, 1999.

Matthee, Rudi, Willem Floor, and Patrick Clawson. *The Monetary History of Iran: from the Safavids to the Qajars*. London: I. B. Tauris, 2013.

Melville, Charles. "From Qars to Qandahar: the Itineraries of Shah 'Abbas I (995–1038/1587–1629)," in *Etudes Safavides*, ed. Jean Calmard, 195–224. Paris and Tehran: L'Institut français de Recherche en Iran, 1993.

INDEX